"And the grace of our Lord w
with faith and love whic
1st Timothy 1
"But where sin abounded, grace ...
Romans 5:20 (AV)

Abundant and Abounding

REV JACKSON C BUICK
WITH GEORGE L GILLESPIE

ISBN 0-9515637-7-7

First published in 2001
by Burning Bush Publications
134, Ballynahinch Road
Lisburn, N. IRELAND
BT27 5HB

Printed and bound in Great Britain by
Edenderry Print Limited
Agnes Street, Belfast, N. IRELAND

CONTENTS

ACKNOWLEDGEMENTS

This publication would not have been possible without the help and support of many people. My indebtedness to them all is immense.

First, I sincerely thank my wife, Daisy, for her unfailing patience and constant encouragement, also for her practical help in researching photographs.

I discussed the book line by line with George L Gillespie. By revising and editing, and running the script off on his wordprocessor, he co-operated enthusiastically as we brought the book to its final format. To him, I am most grateful, also to his wife, June, for her hospitality in their Larne home and her understanding as I stole her husband for so many hours.

I am much obliged to Mrs Anne McNie for undertaking so cheerfully the tedious proof-reading of the manuscript, and for her helpful suggestions.

I am also deeply indebted to the Rev David Temple and his secretary, Mrs Mandy Higgins, in the Irish Mission Office for help in preparing the material for printing.

The cover design is the joint effort of the Rev John McCullough and Rev David J. Temple. John McCullough gave invaluable advice about the illustrations. To him and to his wife, Morag, I express my heartfelt gratitude.

I appreciate very much the willingness of the Very Rev Dr S John Dixon, minister of First Antrim Presbyterian Church, to write a foreword to the book.

During the last nine months I have consulted many others who have been unfailingly considerate in answering queries and providing information. To all these, especially those who provide the written testimonies at the end, I say a final thank-you.

J. C. Buick

FOREWORD

I believe it was Hudson Taylor who said, '*God is looking for men small enough for Him to use.*' Jackson Buick would not presume to any sense of earthly greatness or intellectual erudition but has told his story to bear testimony to the greatness of God. It should stand as an incentive to any of us to realise that availability to God and obedience to his requirements are the only prerequisites to a spiritually fruitful life.

Privileged as I am to serve the Lord in First Antrim Presbyterian Church, Daisy's and Jackson's home congregation, I realise the lasting impact his life has had on our people. Indeed, since their going out to service, a steady stream of young people have followed into missionary work, city mission ministry and the ordained ministry of our church.

Jackson's ministry, however, took him into a very specialised situation in 1982. At a time in our history when Northern Ireland's prisons were very busy, he became a significant witness to a group not always popular in society or even the church. He faithfully and relevantly confronted wrongdoers with the inevitable consequences of their sin, while holding out for all to embrace the love, mercy, and grace of God. No less importantly he reminded the respectable, law-abiding churchgoers to be Christ-like in their attitude to prisoners.

Jackson Buick remains an inspiration to all who know him. I consider it an honour to be associated with his ministry over the decades. It is my prayer that many will read this account of God's work in and through him and be inspired and challenged as a result to yield themselves to God with the same ready obedience and steady faithfulness that shines through these pages. May it be so to the Glory of our great God.

The Very Revd Dr S John Dixon

PREFACE

The Rev Jackson Buick cuts his hedges on a breezy day. This means that when it comes to the tidying up, he has help from the wind in disposing of the leaves. Jackson Buick has that knack. With a blend of infectious exuberance and adroit timing he has a way of enlisting the help of all and sundry, the elements included.

Initially I was a reluctant conscript. But as I started, and then continued, to work with him on this book I came to enjoy the process and profit from it. Jackson still produced the leaves, this time paper (not tree) ones. Perhaps because of an early, necessary lesson in 'waste not, want not,' these leaves turned out to be a fascinating assortment of circulars, agendas, rotas, schedules and duplicated letters. By using the blank sides of these, Jackson was able to pen or pencil his reminiscences. He then posted or brought them straight to me. Like the wind, I then helped with the 'tidying up.'

I soon discovered that there was more to this man than I already knew from his time in the 1970's as minister of the congregation where my wife and I worshipped. During those years he made a deep impression on the people of Craigy Hill Presbyterian Church. His preaching was evangelical, forthright and down-to-earth. Significantly, it was on a wavelength to which people could easily tune to receive the message. Pastorally, Jackson had the ability to get alongside those for whom life had not been a bed of roses. In the middle of a crowd he had the capacity to make each feel noticed and important. 'Boss' was a frequent form of address he used. As I think of Jackson I am often reminded of words that were applied to Christ: '*The common people heard Him gladly.*'

(Mark 12:37).

I remember sitting beside him during a meeting of the General Assembly when a Doctor of Philosophy was holding forth in a speech liberally spiced with theological and sociological jargon. Very simply Jackson turned to me and said, 'I don't understand one word he's talking about.' I suspect that few of those who politely applauded understood either. It was typical of Jackson. He makes no pretence of being what he is not.

As these reflections reveal, Jackson does not fit into the usual pattern of Presbyterian ministry. Whether at Larne or Letterkenny, in home or hospital, with converts or convicts, Jackson Buick is the sort of person around and to whom things are constantly happening.

This book does not set out to be a discourse on theology; nonetheless many interesting theological considerations arise from it. Nor does it set out to be an exhaustive treatise of God's dealings with human beings. While the basics of Christianity remain constant, the manner in which those basics are outworked varies according to an individual's personality, background and circumstances. Many will be able to relate to one or more of the conversion stories described inside these covers; others will have had their own distinct but still valid encounters with Christ. Within the boundaries of religion there are many different authentic - as well as counterfeit - Christian professions. It would be a cause for rejoicing in heaven if this book helped someone, who is not a Christian, to repent and be genuinely born again of the Spirit.

Again, although the book is not intended to be a formal autobiography, it is essentially autobiographical, being a selection of the incidents and people that have embellished Jackson Buick's long and - at eighty years of age - still active life. Towards the end some Christians - including his wife Daisy

- record, or have recorded for them, thumbnail autobiographical sketches.

Was it not Winston Churchill who described Clement Attlee as 'a humble man with plenty to be humble about.'? This witty knocking of one prime minister by another might, I think, be accepted by Jackson Buick as a description of himself, not in a Uriah Heepish way but as a description of how he considers himself. He makes no secret of his humble beginnings, nor of his education owing more to the university of life than to any institute of learning or college of theology. As for his gifts - and remarkable they are - he attributes these totally to the grace of God. This is what he wants this book to be - a narrative of God's abundant and abounding grace in his own life and in the lives of others.

To God be the glory!
Great things He hath done!

George L Gillespie

Chapter 1

Births and Deaths

Rover, Hotspur, Beano, Dandy: in my childhood these words were magic, for they were the comics eagerly awaited in households throughout Northern Ireland and beyond. For some reason, however, reading about the exploits of Desperate Dan and Pansy Potter, the Strong Man's daughter had little appeal for me. One thing I did read fairly regularly - though again without much enthusiasm - was the Children's Page in The Christian Herald. The motto of the Golden Star Brigade was 'Look up and aim high.' Old fashioned as it may now seem, this motto was probably not without influence on a developing mind. Apart from the Herald the only other weekly paper to come into our humble home was the Ballymena Weekly. There was neither time for reading nor money for buying luxuries like books and magazines.

A book that did grip my attention was *The Swiss Family Robinson,* an early Sunday School prize. Written by the 19th century Berne pastor, J D Wyss, it described the adventures of four brothers - Fritz, Franz, Ernest and Jack - and their parents when they were shipwrecked on an uninhabited island. I was fascinated.

As I take up the pen to describe my adventures and, thankfully, minus the shipwreck I do so with a very real sense of my absolute inadequacies, misgivings and shortcomings. If it had not been for the constant prodding and encouragement of many friends, I could never have started to share these experiences of my journey through life. Indeed, to go much further, had it not been for the grace of God and the enabling of His Holy Spirit, I would probably long since have been on the scrap heap of humanity. If this book does in fact get completed, my sincere wish is that it will bring glory to the One who saved me and loosed me from my sins.

As I reflect on the years that are gone, many faces flit before my mind's eye. These belong to individuals who played a part in shaping and moulding my character. Their witness to, and work for, God have inspired me, and enhanced my life and ministry. I have asked a few of them to share their experiences of God's grace in their lives and I am sure that their contributions will prove a blessing.

But I must begin at the beginning. I first saw the light of day at Creavery, Randalstown, County Antrim. There, on the 8 October 1921 - not long after the birth of the state of Northern Ireland - I was born, the youngest of three children of George and Margaret Buick. My mother's maiden name was Warwick. I was given the name Jackson Crawford. My parents' first child was my elder brother, James. Sadly at the age of seven years he died

My parents seem to have had more than their fair share of both employment and financial problems. So they moved to Scotland where, for a time, my father worked in the coal mines. It was backbreaking - sometimes heartbreaking - work, but the wages were good.

During their time in Glasgow my sister, Georgina (Ina for short), was born. Eventually she was to become Mrs Morrison and the mother of the Rev Colin Morrison now minister of Eglinton Presbyterian Church in Belfast. On 17th October 2000 she died of motor neurone disease. Throughout this progressive, degenerative illness Ina retained a radiant faith in Jesus Christ. Even as she became increasingly dependent on others, she remained a bright witness to the grace of God in her life. But again my thoughts are taking me on ahead of myself.

Scotland did not remain their abode for long. Northern Ireland beckoned the family back. My father bought a small farm near Antrim. But his days of farming were cut short, for in 1928 he died leaving my mother with the responsibility of bringing up my sister and me on her own. Because I was then only seven years of age, my memories of my father are few; for this reason they are all the more treasured. For instance, I remember sitting on his knee when neighbours or friends would be in for a good night's crack.

My father's illness lasted only a few months. From across the years there comes back to me another image - faintly remembered but real - of going into the sick room and speaking to my father, and some days later of being taken aside by a neighbour and told that he had died.

On the day of the funeral the Minister and Clerk of Session arrived, also friends and neighbours. The Rev Matthew Majury, minister of First Antrim Presbyterian Church from 1920 until 1961, conducted the service in the home.

The coffin with my father's remains was set in the yard outside the front door. Then men came alongside. Solemnly and silently they bore the coffin away on their shoulders.

It seems to me that I just accepted death as an intrinsic part of the human fabric. Nor had the grim reaper finished with our household yet. Exactly a month after my father's departure, my grandfather Warwick, who had been living with us, also died and was buried from our home. Just how death plays upon a child's mind is hard to say, but these early reminders of man's mortality were no doubt used by God to help mould me into the man I became.

A few paragraphs ago I intimated that my mother brought us up by herself. This was true only from the human viewpoint for she, like Enoch, walked with God. What I owe to my mother I can never put into words. Hers was a quiet, sincere faith. So far as I know she never stood on a public platform nor addressed a crowd but her life spoke more eloquently than many sermons. In the privacy of the home she took her baptismal vows seriously, seeking to bring Ina and myself up in the fear and admonition of the Lord. Always she instilled into us respect for others. Tittle-tattle, gossip and character assassination were out. From her I learned to look for the best in people and to encourage, not condemn, them.

Between the First and Second World wars there was no system of social security such as was to develop after 1947. For widows and orphans life was lived close to - sometimes below - the breadline.

After my father's death the total weekly income to our home was eighteen shillings - 90 pence in today's money. On Mondays my mother went to neighbouring farmhouses to do a day's washing and cleaning. For her day's labour she received half-a-crown. (It took eight of these to make £1.) In the Spring she helped with the planting of crops; in the

Autumn she helped with harvesting. In more senses than one, seed time and harvest did not cease, for, with mechanisation not yet widespread, the space between these two seasons was very short.

My mother did not send us to our church, First Antrim Presbyterian, which was about two and a half miles away; she took us there. My sister was first to get a bicycle, so she was all right, but until I also got one, I had to sit on the carrier of my mother's bicycle. My mother did not believe in buying anything before she was able to pay for it in full.

Outside the home, faithful Sunday School teachers were an influence for good. It was not simply their teaching but, perhaps even more, their way of life that left its mark on me. I also owe a lot to Mr McKittrick, the principal of Shane's Castle Elementary School which I attended. This man ran an afternoon Sunday School where I learned about Joseph and his coat of many colours, David and Goliath, Daniel in the den of lions and much else.

JACKSON'S MOTHER

JACKSON'S FATHER

Spheres of Ministry of Rev. Jackson Buick

BCM

Belfast City Mission - 1944 to 1956

Second Newtownards Presbyterian Church 1963 to 1970

Chapter 2

Conversation and Conversion

When I reached 14 years of age, I started work in the Old Bleach Linen Company in Randalstown. Although I was still attending church and Bible class, also reading my Bible and saying my prayers, there was a void in my life. At work I wanted to be one of the boys, so swearing and filthy stories became a way of life for me. It was a Jekyll-Hyde existence - good on Sunday, not so good on Monday, worse on Tuesday. This made me unhappy.

Around this time Miss Beth Porter and Miss Margaret Smith formed a Young People's Fellowship in First Antrim Presbyterian Church. It met in the Church Hall on a Saturday night providing a meeting place for young people whose Saturday night pastime otherwise consisted of walking around the streets in groups. The programme was simple, unsophisticated by later standards. Games, quizzes and fun were followed by light refreshments, singing of choruses and, finally, an epilogue.

On my very first night at this Youth Fellowship a young lady gave her testimony. This was something new to me; but it struck a chord. Like me, this young lady had the habit of daily reading the Bible and saying her prayers. Like me, she had been unhappy and dissatisfied. In her testimony she told how in a personal encounter with Christ she had surrendered her life to Him.

What she said troubled my conscience. A voice within me seemed to say, 'Jackson, that is what you need.' Over the next sixteen months this voice kept prompting me. Frequently, but especially on a Sunday night, I would kneel at my bedside. With sincerity I would tell the Lord I was a sinner and ask Him to save me. Of course I promised to stop swearing and the like. I might - or might not - get through Monday, but by Tuesday I was back to my old ways.

Saturday 11th November, 1938 was a Remembrance Day I was never to forget. That night I was standing at a bus stop in Antrim with Beth Porter who was waiting for a bus to take her to Belfast. We began to talk. The conversation was short but to the point. Miss Porter addressed me in a very direct manner. 'Jackson,' she asked, 'are you a Christian?'

I answered, 'No,' then added, 'but I would like to be.' And I explained how, despite my bedside prayers, nothing seemed to happen.

'Jackson,' replied Miss Porter, 'when you ask the Lord to save you, believe that He has done it.'

I just looked up towards heaven and quietly said, 'Lord, I don't know what it is to believe but I do believe.'

Just then the bus arrived, Miss Porter stepped onto it and was gone. There had been no standing up in a meeting, no putting up of a hand, no counselling - in fact it was just as I have described it. That night, however, when I returned home, I spoke to my mother about trusting the Lord.

Monday morning arrived. I was in a group of men when one of them told a filthy story. I probably laughed with the others but for the first time in my life I did not enjoy that story. I just wanted to get away from their company.

For the week after my conversion I was not at work. When I did return, it was not long until I was challenged.

About 9.00 am one of my Old Bleach Linen Company mates said, 'Buick, you have been in work for an hour and I haven't heard you swear yet. What's up?'

I replied that I had got converted Saturday night week ago. Laughing, the rest said, 'We will give you a fortnight to keep it.'

The usual banter followed. In their eyes I was a hypocrite, to be made fun of. For the next few weeks two of them would push me into a small cloakroom where we hung our coats. There, out of sight, they used me as a punchball. At times my arms were so sore I could hardly lift them. My mates' aim was to get me to swear. By God's grace I was able to cope.

One incident stands out. I was holding a beaker into which a workmate was pouring sulphuric acid. Some of it spilled over my hand. So sharp and intense was the pain that I involuntarily yelped, taking God's name in vain. Immediately I was overcome with anxiety. What would I do when my workmate told the other boys? I would not be able to deny that I had sworn. My profession of faith would be discredited.

In my turmoil I went back into the cloakroom, this time by myself. Here is the gist of the prayer I uttered, 'Lord, You know what has happened. I cannot deny that I have taken Your Name in vain. I fear that under hassle from the boys I will cave in. But, Lord, I don't want to cave in. Lord, I am in Your hands.'

The extraordinary thing is that the workmate who had spilled the acid never breathed a word about how I had blotted my copybook. It was not that he was any friend of mine. On the contrary he seldom missed an opportunity to tease me and accuse me of hypocrisy. In those early days the outcome of this incident was a great help to me. Somehow it seemed that God had undertaken for me.

Commitment to Christ soon led to me becoming more involved in the work of First Antrim Presbyterian Church. I was given a class in the afternoon Sunday School. Two years later when, for health reasons, the superintendent had to resign, I took over from him.

I also became the lookout convener in First Antrim's Young People' Christian Endeavour which at that time was a thriving organisation. My task was to seek new members. In my naivety and enthusiasm I remember visiting a young man in his home and issuing an ultimatum. I was not going to leave until he promised to come to the CE. God overruled my impulsiveness. John did come to the CE. John did much more than that. As I write he is still one of First Antrim's senior elders.

CE gave me many opportunities to put my faith into practice. It was in CE that I first prayed in public and first chaired any sort of meeting. A feature that required organisation was the Sunshine Visit. Four CE members would visit those in the congregation who could not easily get out and about. In the home the four would conduct a little service. One would act as chairperson, others would sing a solo, read the Scriptures and give a 5-10 minute talk. On these Sunshine Visits I made my first attempts at a sermon. The first full service I conducted was the weekly Sunday afternoon service in Oldstone

Faith Mission Hall.

It is hard for me to praise the Christian Endeavour too highly. To me it was - still is - the finest organisation for training and equipping young people for Christian growth and work. Opportunities abounded. First Antrim CE met with other CEs. On Summer Sunday evenings we joined with High Street Church CE for open air meetings in Antrim's Market Square. Along with the others, I got experience of outreach work. The passers-by saw us in the group, hence we were making an open confession of Christ.

At the second of these open-airs I had to lead the service. A member brought a box out from a grocer's yard for me to stand on. I did not like this one little bit. I had no desire to be called a soapbox preacher. Nor was my embarrassment lessened when I spied from my raised position on the box those workmates who had become the bane of my life. There they were, waving their fists at me. I wished that a hole would open in the ground and swallow me up there and then.

Afterwards it was different, very different. The teasing and fun-making continued but from that day on never again was I in the slightest embarrassed to profess that I was a Christian. It was as if God used this mocking to mature and strengthen me. After all these years I can affirm in all honesty that I am thankful for those days. Far from making me doubt, these testings validated the foundation on which my Christian faith was built.

Spheres of Ministry of Rev. Jackson Buick (continued)

Craigy Hill Presbyterian Church
1970 to 1982

Crumlin Road Prison Chaplain
1982 to 1990

Chapter 3

Flax factory and Mission hall

While all these events in my Christian life were unfolding I continued to be employed in the Old Bleach. There is no point in pretending that I liked my work there. It was therefore with a certain amount of relief that I changed my place of employment. I joined the staff of the Flax Processing Factory Spinning Company at Muckamore. What a change! Now I began to enjoy work especially when I was appointed to travel with the boss, and sometimes on my own, around the farming community. These were the years when Northern Ireland was just about the most important flax-growing region of the United Kingdom and Irish linen was prized worldwide. My job now was to use my powers of persuasion to encourage farmers to grow flax for our firm. I also had the responsibility for marketing the finished flax and seed. As I journeyed to the weekly markets in Ballymena and Magherafelt, I had many interesting encounters.

Not surprisingly my Christian principles were often tested. On one occasion I found myself in the room of a bar in Magherafelt where, naturally enough, farmers and seed merchants were consuming alcohol. I refused either to drink the stuff myself or to buy it for others. As an alternative I invited them for a meal wondering all the time if I had enough money to pay for it. As we said our farewells a farmer said to me, 'I admire you for your courage and convictions.' In small ways like this, God proved that His grace was sufficient.

Those were great days indeed. I loved my work in the factory. I enjoyed my work with the young people of First Antrim. The minister, the Rev Matthew Majury (to be awarded a doctorate in 1954), was a real Barnabas. Many other church leaders also encouraged me.

In the 1920s the state had taken over - not without controversy - church day schools. First Antrim had several old schoolhouses and in those at Lady Hill, Rathmore and Oldstone Sunday evening services were conducted by elders and other gifted men. I, too, was given the privilege of officiating and this gave me experience for later in life.

Something else of great significance now took place. Genesis 2:24 reads, 'Therefore shall a man leave his father and mother, and cleave unto his wife: and they shall be one flesh.' On 9th July1943 this verse became a reality as Margaret Jane McDowell and I were married in First Antrim Presbyterian Church. Daisy - as my wife is better known - was a member of First Antrim choir, the Girls' Auxiliary and of course the Christian Endeavour. She often sang solos at church functions and meetings. One of her favourites was *The Old Rugged Cross.*

The hymn is a poignant, personal statement of faith:-

I will cling to the old rugged cross
Till my trophies at last I lay down;
I will cherish the old rugged cross
And exchange it some day for a crown.

Over the years Daisy and I have shared that faith in Christ crucified on Calvary's cross. Throughout my ministry I have leaned on my wife for guidance in anything musical and, if truth be told, in much else. In the work of the Belfast City Mission (where we were shortly to go) and in the various congregations (where we went later) Daisy was a constant source of strength. In Sunday Schools, Children's meetings and the Presbyterian Women's Association, in providing hospitality and in the entire work of the Kingdom Daisy took a leading part. And yes, we still cling to that old rugged cross, and look forward to exchanging it some day for a Crown.

As a young Christian I met a man who was to touch my life crucially. This was David Hamilton, now dead, who in the 1940's joined the Belfast City Mission, eventually becoming its Executive Secretary. He invited me to Belfast for a weekend and I preached at his Sunday evening services. About this time Christian friends in Antrim suggested that I, too, should apply for the Belfast City Mission.

I prayed. I pondered. Then I took the first tentative steps. From the initial approach until receipt of the application form took five or six weeks. It was during this somewhat protracted period that my factory manager, Mr Ferguson Grainger, called me into his office. He shared some of the hopes and plans he had for me within the firm. The future looked bright. If I responded positively I had a secure job doing what I loved with every prospect of a comfortable - even prosperous life style. Since no reply had come from the Belfast City Mission I thought that a life in business was God's plan for me. When the application form did arrive I tossed it into a drawer from where it was as likely as not to be consigned to the waste paper bin.

Just as it seemed my future was assured I had a slight accident. About 11 o'clock one Saturday morning I was throwing a one hundredweight bag of corn onto my shoulder when my foot slipped. I stumbled, tearing muscles and ligaments in my neck. So severe was the pain that I all but fainted. I struggled home and into bed. I looked at the clock. I remember distinctly the time: 11.30 am. Despite the pain, which remained almost unbearable, my thoughts for some reason turned again to the application form for Belfast City Mission. It was still in the drawer. 'Lord,' I prayed, 'if you take away this pain before 12:00 noon I'll fill in that form.' By noon the pain had gone. Although for about a week I could not straighten my neck, the pain did not return.

Within a few days I filled in the application form. Like Martin Luther, I could do no other, and like him, too, I thought, 'So help me God', for deep down I was apprehensive, almost hoping nothing would come of it. But something did come of it. Soon I was preaching a trial sermon in McClure Street Mission Hall. I do not remember what my text was. I only know that by 7.45 pm I could go on no longer. So much for all my careful preparation! A service of three quarters of an hour was far short of what I thought would satisfy the Director of the Belfast City Mission.

Next morning - Monday - I was back in the factory. Mr Grainger wanted to speak to me again. He was setting up a project in which I could be his partner. A similar project the previous year had made a profit of £400 (roughly a labourer's annual wage); the new project was to be much bigger. That meant a bigger profit, half of which would come to me and be in addition to my normal salary.

When I told Mr Grainger about my application he wanted me, if I was accepted, to request the Belfast City Mission to allow me to continue with the York Street Spinning Company until October 1944 when the project would be complete.

The morning before I left for my interview Mr Grainger spoke yet again. 'Jackson,' he concluded, 'if you stay with me I'll double your wages.' Even before this promised rise my salary would have fallen by about 30 shillings per week by going to the city.

My interview with the Belfast City Mission Directors went quite well, I thought. So, too, must they, for at the end the President said to me, 'There is a hall in Ligoniel to which we are happy to appoint you. If you refuse to accept that appointment your name will be removed from our books. Of course you can reapply but there is no guarantee we would consider you.'

Like my employer, the President was in the flax business. 'Remember,' he added, ''that there is a greater need for City Missionaries than for flax buyers.'

Having asked the Directors for a week to make up my mind, I left the interview and met Daisy who was in business in Belfast. We talked through the turn of events over a meal. For both of us it was a stressful time. We were just married, we were setting up a home, we liked the countryside. Personally I still loved my work in York Street and, to be honest, I had ambitions of climbing the business ladder and in the process seeing Europe - Belgium and Holland in particular. Why should I give up the prospect of a comfortable, secure career? I also knew that I had to make up my mind quickly.

In her quiet, sincere way Daisy felt that the City Mission was the place of God's appointment. So in my bones did I. Our decision was made. We returned to the Belfast City Mission office to accept the post at Ligoniel Hall. When Mr

William Wylie, Executive Secretary, heard the news he took my hand and said, 'There is no higher calling than the calling of God; there is no greater work than the work of the Kingdom.' Then he added, 'None of God's seed will ever beg bread.'

To that last remark I can say 'Amen.' Even when the cash was short we were never reduced to begging. There comes back to me the memory of a night in a Mission Hall 6 miles from Ballymena. After the service I had to pay taxi, bus and tram fares which left me with only a few pence in my pocket - but I had been able to get home. In those days no travelling expenses were given. 'Religion on the cheap,' might well have been the comment of a now deceased ministerial friend, the Rev Tom Cuming.

Having decided to become a City Missioner I still had to face Mr Grainger. This I did the day after my appointment. My new bosses had refused the request for an extension of my time with his Company. Mr Grainger was certainly disappointed, probably hurt, and possibly angry. Be that as it may, until he died we exchanged Christmas cards and occasionally I called to see him. But my employment at the Flax Factory terminated. The date was 29 February 1944.

DAISY'S MOTHER

DAISY'S FATHER

Chapter 4

Ballysillan and Legoniel

On 1st March 1944 I began my new life. At a Service of Induction in the City Mission Hall on the Ligoniel Road I was introduced to the people of Ballysillan and Ligoniel. Taking part was the Rev Dr Herbert Vere Clements who was reputed to be 'of sound scholarship, wise judgment, and a devoted pastor.' From 1927 until his death in 1954 he ministered in Ballysillan Presbyterian Church which I now started to attend on Sunday mornings. Also participating in the Induction were the Rev Matthew Majury, from First Antrim (where I had learned so much) and Mr William Wylie, Executive Secretary of the Belfast City Mission (where I had it all to learn).

It is curious how the details of a past event - even a personal one - can slip almost completely from the memory yet with one detail of it remaining as clear as a star that twinkles brightly long after others have dimmed. What lingers uniquely in my memory from that evening in 1944 is the singing of Metrical Psalm121.

I to the hills will lift mine eyes,
From whence doth come mine aid,
My safety cometh from the Lord,
Who heaven and earth hath made.

As I lifted my eyes to the craggy hills to the north and west of Belfast, it seemed as if this psalm had been written specifically for this place and for this time. Daily I was ascending and descending the steepish inclines of Ligoniel. Starting out on my new mission field, I was conscious of how much 'mine aid' depended on Him 'who heaven and earth hath made.'

For two decades my predecessor, William Cumings, had tramped these streets as a missionary. By 1944, however, he had already been gone for two years to his new posting in Hemsworth Street off the Shankill Road. During this interlude a faithful core of twenty or so people from the Ligoniel Hall continued the Sunday and Thursday night meetings.

In Ballysillan and Ligoniel I was following a relatively short line of missionaries. In 1914 the first of these, Ernest A Barr, started a Sunday School in Emerson's Row and Gospel meetings in Wolfhill Schoolroom. Over the following years different venues were used until finally the hall at Ligoniel was settled on. Into this goodly heritage I now entered.

Here was I, a country boy, from the backwoods of County Antrim, trying to find his preaching bearings in the city where in the previous century the Rev Dr Henry Cooke had held the Presbyterian Assembly spellbound and where the Rev Dr Hugh Hanna (Roaring Hugh) had held forth in St Enoch's in which, shortly after my induction, the Rev Austin Fulton was installed.

Belfast had hatched many great preachers, past and present. In my fledgling enthusiasm I set out not to emulate any but simply to be myself.

On 2nd March I had my introduction to pastoral visitation. William Cumings accompanied me on a few calls to homes in the district. My preparation course had combined theory and practice in one neat afternoon package. On 3rd March I was knocking doors by myself.

The mission, of which I was now a part, dated back to 1827. The early nineteenth century saw the building not only of mills and factories but also streets of terraced housing for the new workers. As people migrated into Belfast from all over rural Ulster they were leaving behind a whole way of life. Away from their ties to land and church, many drifted away from Christianity.

Into this situation came the Rev Reuben John Bryce. One of the distinguished sons of the Rev James Bryce (who in 1816 became a founding member of the Associate Presbytery of Ireland), Reuben was Principal of the Belfast Academy. Now, with others of like mind, he formed the Belfast Town (later City) Mission whose purpose was 'the promotion of Christ's cause among the poor, the careless and the Churchless.'

The first agent was William Cochrane. Described by the Rev Dr James Morgan, the first minister of Fisherwick as 'one of the mightiest instruments for good that Belfast ever saw,' William Cochrane died prematurely 'worn down and seized with fever.' One hundred years later diseases like tuberculosis, scarlet fever, measles and diphtheria were still a scourge especially among the poor.

Like their ancestors, the people among whom I was now ensconced as a Christian pastor in 1944 were often poor in material terms but rich in character and resourcefulness. In view of later events it is not without significance to note that the Belfast City Mission sometimes provided a route by which men proceeded into the full-time ministry. However it took many years before that thought was to enter my mind.

Nor was I to know then that another venture with which I was to be associated in later years had its origins in the same year as I became a City Missionary. For young men who had got into trouble with the law - Belfast apprentices in particular - a Boys' Residential Club was opened. It had to close in 1974 but reopened 10 years later in W J Thompson Memorial House. How this impinged on my life will transpire later.

In the Spring of 1944 the war was still thundering on, its end still more than a year away. For one week in February London suffered the heaviest air raids for almost three years. In March United States bombers began daylight attacks on Berlin. For its part Belfast continued to suffer from the repercussions of the devastating German air raids of April and May 1941. With rebuilding at a virtual standstill, housing was scarce. As the City Mission did not provide accommodation for its missionaries, Daisy and I had no option but to live with others, seldom a prospect that is anticipated with delight.

Our first stop was with a couple at 92 Velsheda Park in the middle of the Ardoyne which a few decades later was to be the focus of so much media attention. After six weeks we moved to 270 Ligoniel Road. Here Miss Esther Stewart and Mrs Agnes McKeown, a widow whose son, William, was a minister in a Presbyterian church in Niagara Falls, Canada, made us feel at home. They were sisters. Daisy and I were treated as part of the family. So close was the relationship that it extended into the next generation. The Canadian McKeowns and Ulster Buicks frequently traversed the Atlantic in both directions. The Rev William McKeown is now dead, but to this day we keep in touch with his widow.

While we were living with these sisters, an expected event

occurred - unexpectedly. I well remember coming back to 270 Ligoniel Road about 10.00 o'clock one Monday evening and the door being locked for the night, so we thought. How wrong we were! One moment we were about to retire, the next we were calling a taxi. Daisy was rushed into the Whitehall Nursing Home on the Antrim Road where next day, Tuesday 17th June 1947, she gave birth to a healthy baby boy weighing 8lbs 4 oz (approx. 3.5kgs). He was our first - and, as it turned out, last - born.

A few days later the Rev H V Clements, living up to the 'good pastor' epithet, took Mrs McKeown and me to the Nursing Home to bring Daisy and the baby home. With obvious pride Mrs McKeown carried Raymond George Buick from the car and placed him in his little cot. Until her death she treated Raymond like a grandson. Her son William went as far as to say that Raymond meant more to his mother than either he or his two sons did. To Raymond, Agnes was Granny McKeown, and Esther, Aunt Essie. 'Granny' and 'aunt' took delight in observing Raymond start to walk and talk and go to school, first to Everton Primary, then to the Boys' Model Secondary. When Esther died, Granny McKeown came to live with us, but by then we had moved to the Second Newtownards manse.

It is hard to overestimate the debt we owe these two sisters. They shared not only in the blessing that comes from Gospel ministry but also in the routine work of the City Mission.

By living among the people - not commuting in and out - we were soon a part of, not apart from, them. Out on the street, waiting at a bus stop or actually on the bus - for we had no car - I was mixing with the people of my district, sharing conversation as well as a seat with them. My previous experience of bereavement, lack of money and the hurly-burly of work meant that I had been where many of them had been. Each weekday as Daisy journeyed to and from work in the city centre, she, too, was making contacts and building relationships. Only a few hundred yards down from where we lived was the Mission Hall. The people who came to the meetings on Sunday were the ones whom we were as likely as not to meet on their way to and from shopping or work on Monday.

All the time our antennae were picking up the vibes of the area, getting to know the hopes and disappointments of the residents of these neatly kept terraced houses. The early visit to the sick bed at home or hospital was often repaid by an appearance at the mission hall. As visitation extended from Ligoniel (which means the hollow of the O'Neill) half-a-mile down the road to Ballysillan (which means the townland of the wild cherries), attendance at both Sunday and Thursday night meetings increased.

By September 1944 my continual stomping around the streets was bringing business for the cobbler. Steel-tipped heels delayed the interval between shoe repairs but made too loud a click-clack along hospital corridors and had to be abandoned. More important was a growing awareness of the spiritual business that lay ahead. The fields were '*white already to harvest;*' Winter lay ahead. What should our Winter labourers be doing? It was time once more to seek the Lord of the Harvest.

Gradually the way ahead became clear. For the first three weeks in January 1945 it was decided to have an evangelistic mission with Mr William Wylie as the evangelist. He was a well-built man with a penchant for forthright speech. Like W P Nicholson, under whose preaching he had been converted, he was the sort of man around whom stories accumulated. In Tyrone he is said to have warned a congregation that they were on the road to Hell with a catechism in one hand and the Presbyterian hymn book in the other. In County Down preaching on the Fall, he is alleged to have thumped the pulpit Bible and bellowed, presumably for double emphasis, '*Adam, where art thou?*' Startled from his drowsy lethargy a man at the back of the congregation stood up and shouted back, 'Here I am.'

In preparation for the mission with this forceful preacher, extra prayer meetings were held. We went around the doors with leaflets. Those who were already Christians invited family members, friends and workmates to the New Year Mission. The time of waiting might be summed up in lines from Metrical Psalm130:

I wait for God, my soul doth wait,
My hope is in his word.
More than they that for morning watch,
My soul waits for the Lord;

Yea, even more than they that watch
The morning light to see.
Let Israel in Jehovah hope,
For with him mercies be;

Redemption also plenteous
Is ever found with him.
And from all his iniquities
He Israel shall redeem.

Young men from the Mission Hall at Newcastle in 1947.
TOMMY GRANT starred left
JOE McDONALD starred centre

Chapter 5

Revival and Revelry

Only eternity will reveal .... In evangelical circles these words often preface remarks made after a mission or word of witness. They combine an uncertainty about what God has accomplished with a certainty that He has fulfilled His purpose. It is true of course that the secret things belong unto the Lord (Deuteronomy 29:29) and that of the four kinds of ground on which the Sower's seed fell, only one was described as good (Luke 8). It is also true that God is pleased to let the redeemed be known by their fruit (Matthew 7:15). That knowledge may become known quickly, or only after many years.

The 1945 Mission was a time during which visible signs followed the preaching of God's Word. As William Wylie proclaimed the Gospel, sinners were saved and backsliders reclaimed. It was a time of blessing indeed.

It was almost 50 years later before one story came to light - at least to me. One day in 1994 - I am not exactly sure of the date - my phone rang. The call was from a man called Harry McDonald. Harry spoke not of himself but of his brother, Joe, who was ill. Joe wanted me to come to see him. I readily agreed.

Joe's story was worth hearing. In his family were three sisters and one brother. Unfortunately his parents were drinkers - out at the pub every Friday and Saturday night. In 1945 a woman in a pub was as uncommon sight as a man in a washtub.

Joe worked in the Bleach Green at Glenbank where he was friendly with Tommy, a bell-ringer at St Marks Parish Church. At work Tommy constantly sang well-known choruses. So infectious was Tommy's bright spirit that Joe could not help asking, ''Tommy, why are you so happy all the time?'

Revealing his secret of salvation Tommy proceeded like this, 'Look Joe, there are special meetings starting at the Mission Hall on the Ligoniel Road. Why don't you go along?'

'I will,' replied Joe, and then, thinking he had agreed too easily, continued, 'but only if I have company, only if my mate, Albert, comes with me.' An unlikely prospect, thought Joe.

But Albert surprised Joe. 'Yes,' was his answer.

On the Tuesday of the first week of the mission the two young men went along to the Ligoniel Hall. Before the service started, they decided they wanted a smoke to carry them through the next hour or so. Off they went to the toilet for their drag on a cigarette.

Coming out of the toilet Joe suddenly stopped. 'We won't bother with the meeting the night, Albert,' he said. 'Let's get out of here. Let's get away home.'

Albert would have none of it. 'We can't do that,' he

retorted. 'Come on, come on, let's get in before it starts.' So in they went.

Next morning Tommy, the bell-ringer, asked how the meeting had gone. 'Will you go back another night?' he queried.

'You can come back to me with your question, but not until the last week of the mission, and we'll see then.' Joe did not want to be badgered.

Knowing the Scriptures, Tommy realized that there was a time to keep a rein on his tongue. His silence lasted as long as Joe requested - until the last week of the Mission. On the Monday of that week he spoke asking if Joe and Albert would be going back to the mission?' They would, and Thursday was the night they chose.

As I visited him in his illness Joe told me what happened. Sitting there in the mission he was made aware of his need. 'Mr Wylie's preaching got to me,' he said.

At the close the preacher issued an invitation. If anyone wished to talk to him about their spiritual need all that was required was to step into the little room behind the pulpit as the closing verse of the last hymn was being sung.

Joe turned to Albert. 'I'm going into that room,' he said. Out into the aisle he stepped..... followed by Albert. 'You don't need to come just because I am,' Joe said, making it easy for his friend to turn back. But Albert kept following. Both went on, together. That night both trusted Christ, together.

For 55 years Joe McDonald bore faithful witness to Christ. A gifted speaker among the Brethren, he was in much demand as a preacher. A lady from one of the Assemblies maintained that nobody knew their Bible better than Joe McDonald.

That was not all. Joe's sisters, brother and boozing parents all came to Christ. One of his three sons is today engaged in personal evangelism in republican areas of Belfast, part of that work being among those with drink and drug problems.

The local Elim Church magazine described the Forty-five Mission as a mini-revival. Certainly it was the spring-board from which the work in Ballysillan and Ligoniel developed. About 50 persons - many with little or no church connection - had passed through the Enquiry Room. At the May Sacrament of the Lord's Supper about 24 - mostly young people -were received into the full fellowship of Ballysillan Presbyterian Church. Fifty-six years later I know of fifteen or so from that time who are still alive and active in churches and fellowships in Belfast.

As the 1945 Winter moved into Spring there was an atmosphere of expectation and excitement. While we tried to organise events, events themselves could create a momentum of their own. The momentum created by VE Day - 8th May 1945 - was overwhelming. Throughout the United Kingdom it was a day of rejoicing and merrymaking.

Belfast celebrated in both religious and secular fashion. Church bells joined with those nationwide in celebration of the defeat of Nazism. Japan still held out but somehow the major enemy seemed to have been defeated. At midday people gathered for a service of prayer and thanksgiving at the City Hall. Churchill's speech was relayed to the crowd after which a group from the armed forces sang:

Praise God from whom all blessings flow;
Praise Him, all creatures here below;
Praise Him above, ye heavenly host;
Praise Father, Son and Holy Ghost.

We in the Ligoniel and Ballysillan could not be left out. In the

Mission Hall we gathered to give our thanks for the victory and offer our prayers for the peace. Belfast had paid a heavy price during the 1941 air raids. Throughout Northern Ireland joy was mixed with sorrow for many who went out to fight for their country would never return.

Festivities of one sort and another continued throughout the whole day. Street parties, sing-songs, music-making with cheering and shouting seemed as if they would never end. I remember individuals with accordions playing as people sang and danced up and down the street. As darkness fell bonfires were lit - Ulster people had plenty of practice at this - and the occasional effigy of Hitler was consigned to the flames.

About fifty of those who had been to the Service of Thanksgiving in the Mission Hall decided to visit one of these bonfires. Our friends and neighbours had already gathered. To go and join them was the natural thing to do for we were bone of their bone and flesh of their flesh.

As these very worldly revelries were in full swing, a suggestion was made that there should be a short service to express openly in the midst of the milling throng our gratitude to God. Taking up the role of choir the group from the Mission Hall stood at the side of an air-raid shelter - one of the many concrete refuges that dotted the city. Men heaved me to the top of the shelter from which vantage point I addressed the people. I recall saying that since we had had days of prayer for deliverance during the war, it was now incumbent upon us to pause and thank God for the peace that had dawned. This we did. The crowd united with the choir in a hymn of praise. I spoke of our indebtedness to those who had made the supreme sacrifice in the front lines and of those who had been killed in the Belfast Blitz. From noisy rollicking the crowd had become hushed and solemn. In prayer I committed all who had lost loved ones to Almighty God and with another hymn brought the service to a close. It had lasted about 20 minutes.

We proceeded to another bonfire ... and another ..... and another before our night was over. At each bonfire we more or less followed the same pattern as at the first. At our final location the crowd approached 400 in number. Even among those who might have been very little time for Christianity there was a desire to be associated with the acknowledgement that God who had been '*our help in ages past*' was also '*our hope for years to come.*' Maybe because of the way in which we identified with them in these VE celebrations some began to come along to our meetings. At any rate attendance at the Ligoniel Hall increased.

In his VE day speech the Lord Mayor, Sir Crawford McCullagh, had been down-to-earth. 'Celebrate the victory,' he said, 'and go back to work.' After the exuberance of 8th May it was back to the routine of 9th May - except that the work at Belfast City Mission was seldom routine.

Chapter 6

Out and About

In the 1940s religious activities did not have to compete with Coronation Street or Eastenders, nor with any television, not even yet with the McCooeys on the radio which itself was still something of a luxury. But there were relaxations. In the streets girls skipped to rhymes like:

One, two, buckle my shoe,
Three, four, knock at the door ... and so on.

Boys played conkers and marbles, maybe graduating to cards and pitch-and-toss. Cinemas - the Broadway, Capitol, Duncairn, Classic, Ritz and many more - entertained with Laurel and Hardy, Tarzan and endless cowboy thrillers. A few might go to a play by St John Ervine or George Shields. Irish League football and Dunmore Stadium were other attractions. And there was always the pub. Even so, underlying society, the Christian ethic was thought of as right even when it was not practised.

Open-air meetings were part of the religious landscape. Every Saturday night there was such a meeting in Gresham Street in the centre of Belfast which attracted people from all over the city. Some were attracted simply by the controversial and confrontational nature of these gatherings.

Much more famous for confrontation were the Custom House Steps. During the Dock Strike of 1907 Jim Larkin had addressed tens of thousands from this ready-made rostrum. In 1932 about sixty thousand of the unemployed had attended a monster rally at the same spot. On Sunday afternoons the Customs House used to be an assembly point for people who came from much further afield than Belfast. Politicians and evangelists - often self-styled - proclaimed all sorts of panaceas for mankind. These were the Belfast equivalent of London's Hyde Park Corner orators though lacking any one of quite the stature of the Rev Dr Donald Soper.

This was the atmosphere in which we at the Ligoniel Mission Hall launched our open air meetings which, for the duration of my stay, remained a regular feature of our Summer Programme. A business lady, who had no connection with the City Mission, presented us with a portable amplifying system. Our aim was to keep the amplification loud enough to reach those who wished to listen but subdued enough to avoid annoyance to people in their homes. Mostly we succeeded. Just occasionally mishandling of the equipment resulted in the emission of an ear-piercing shriek. Even so I recollect only one untoward incident. After one mishap with the amplification a young man came fuming down the street cursing - with his volume well turned up - because we had wakened his child.

In our open-air work we planned to cover the Ligoniel

and Ballysillan areas by selecting strategic streets. In most of the streets a percentage of the residents would come and stand at the door. If they were old or frail they sat inside their tiny porches or on warmer evenings in chairs on the street. Afterwards many spoke of their appreciation especially if they were no longer able to attend church.

At the close of one of these meetings I, as usual, thanked those who had listened. Probably I also apologised for any inconvenience caused. Then I concluded something like this: 'If there is anyone within hearing distance who has a problem spiritual or otherwise, do please come and speak to us.'

Inside one home a man who had backslidden was prompted by an inner voice to attend the meeting on the following Sunday night. At the close of that service he rededicated himself to God. More than fifty years later this man still attends the Ligoniel Hall.

Another pastime of the late Forties and early Fifties was walking. Up and down or round and round depending on the street pattern went the walkers, young people in droves on Sunday evenings spilling out over the road where cars were so few that they presented little danger. This walking often occurred after attendance at church. Some said that young people just went to church to meet those of the opposite sex. If so it was no bad place to meet one's future partner. Strangely enough though, in church boys and girls often sat separately, on opposite sides of the gallery if there was one.

Then it was into the walking. I remember watching the crowds of young people walking up the Crumlin Road to Glenbank Corner - up and down, up and down until bedtime.

Our view of all this improved when we moved house. A generous couple - J H Hutchinson and his wife - bought No.793 Crumlin Road and gave it to the Belfast City Mission. Unusually, the Mission now had a property for renting. For the princely rent of one shilling (5p) per year Daisy and I made 793 Crumlin Road our home. This property was situated near Glenbank Corner just beside a shop with a double front at the corner of Glenside Parade and Crumlin Road. Very convenient was the large open space where we could stand and conduct our services.

To make these open-airs interesting and attractive to passers-by we arranged solos, duets and quartets. The singing of old time Gospel favourites was sure to find favour; we were fortunate to have several good singers. In the postwar years with food rationing and general austerity people wanted something to lift their spirits and singing helped. Young people listened to the Top Twenty to which local interest was added when Ruby Murray with hits like ***Softly, softly*** entered the charts. One of our young female singers, Ella Gillespie, was just as good - or so we thought - and so similar in her singing that she could be mistaken for Ruby Murray. This helped to draw the crowds.

Another crowd-puller was William J Morgan. He ran a furniture removal business, represented Oldpark as a very popular Unionist MP and was one of the superintendents of the Belfast City Mission. On the evening he addressed the open-air the crowd multiplied by five or six times, from the usual 40-50 to 250-300. Twice the police had to usher the listeners in off the road.

These then were some of the activities that flowed from the 1945 mission. Those who had made a profession of faith and those who had been revived and renewed in their faith needed to be nurtured and encouraged.

We started a Monday Night Bible Class. Average attendance was eighty with maybe a hundred on the roll. The Christian Endeavour for younger people - mainly under 25 years old - also got under way. As with myself, this proved a training ground for some who went on into a Christian vocation.

For people in those days the annual holiday often consisted of a day at the seaside. It was possible to take the train from Belfast to Bangor and back for a bob (5p). At the City Mission we capitalised on this love of outings. In the Summer we set off on Saturday evenings to Divis, Cavehill or the Giant's Ring.

In 1946 we had a more ambitious project. For a whole week in that Summer I booked two adjacent guest houses (owned by two sisters) in Newcastle, County Down. Daisy and the girls went into one house and I with the boys into the other. For the succeeding eight or nine years similar holidays were arranged - to Portrush, Rhyl in North Wales but especially back time and again to Newcastle.

THE HOLIDAY GROUP AT RHYL

The pattern of these holidays did not vary much. Every morning and evening there was communal prayer. Sometimes the meetings - and the prayers - were brief. It was good to remember that the very brief prayer of the publican - '*Lord be merciful to me a sinner'* - was very effective. Very often we conducted the open-air meetings for which the Faith Mission was responsible. But nobody either inside or outside our group was buttonholed. I suppose lodged somewhere in our psyche was a lesson learned from bellicose evangelists and a memory of James 1:20, '... *the wrath of man worketh not the righteousness of God.'*

Somehow those days seem more distant than their actual fifty years. It was a different world. Young people were easily amused, violence and crime were much rarer than nowadays. There was no morning-after pill, no Brooke clinic, no easy availability of contraceptives. Yet sexual problems were far fewer than they are today. On those holidays we did not have, nor did we need, many rules. Everyone was expected back at the guest houses by 11.00 am, extended to midnight for something like a fireworks display: that was about it.

That this deadline was breached only once - at least to my memory - is a tribute to the sense of responsibility that these postwar young people had. The one infringement of the midnight rule involved a boy whom I shall call Andy - a lovable character who made no pretence of being a Christian. At 12.30 am there was no sign of Andy, nor at 1.00 am, nor yet at 1.30 am. Someone remarked that he had been seen about 11.45 pm heading towards Coleraine (we were at Portrush that year)..... with a girl. By 1.30 am I was ready to explode. I would let him know what was what on his return. I would show him who was boss. At 2.00 am the miscreant returned. He threw his arms around my neck and kissed me three times saying, 'Mr Buick, she loved me like that and I couldn't leave her.' I gave him a bit of a cuff and went to bed without uttering word. There was a sequel: Andy had spoken the truth; unable to leave that girl he took her to be his wife.

A typical week at Ligoniel Mission Hall went like this.

At 9.00 am on Sunday 12 to 20 Christians met for prayer, then went to their own church which, for most, was Ballysillan Presbyterian. The afternoon Sunday School was attended by approximately 120 children taught by a faithful band of dedicated teachers. Between 100 and 120 people gathered for worship at the Sunday evening service. Monday was for the Bible Class, Wednesday for the Christian Endeavour, Thursday for the Fellowship Meeting, and Saturday for the Prayer Meeting which attracted about 50 people. There were no visual aids, no sound effects, in fact no frills of any kind. People just were themselves. After the meetings they were in no hurry home; they sat around in groups chatting and socialising.

From the Mid-Forties to the Mid-Fifties we had an average of more than 50 young people - some leaving, others joining - connected with the hall. Boy met girl; sometimes this led on to wedding bells. Unless my memory is greatly in error not one of these marriages ended in divorce. The old virtues of loyalty and sticking to it through good times and bad still held. This was something for which Daisy and I were profoundly thankful, above all to Almighty God.

The Mission Hall Workers 1945

CHAPTER 7

LATIN AND GREEK

A marriage of ten years is, I am told, entitled to celebrate its tin anniversary, but my ten years at the Belfast City Mission elicited no note of celebration not even from a tin whistle. The First of March 1954 came and went like any other day. During the previous decade there had of course been many days of rejoicing as sinners found or rediscovered new life in Christ. For Daisy and me that was celebration enough.

But if Harold Wilson once described a week as 'a long time in politics,' 520 weeks in the City Mission can hardly be described as short. It was long enough to be able to look back with some satisfaction, yet forward with an inquisitive eye. In a more focussed way I saw that there was a mission field beyond Ligoniel and Ballysillan. At the same time some from that wider arena were eyeing and appraising me.

In May, or perhaps June 1954 the Congregational Church in Ballymena, which was vacant, made an informal approach to me. Would I respond positively if the congregation made out a call to me? Though the exact terms of my reply now escape me, I know that I definitely did not reject the overture out-of-hand. Rather, the matter seems to have been left in limbo and therein lay the problem. I was expecting a further approach from Ballymena but none came. For their part - as I learned much later - the Congregationalists were waiting for word from me. The perverse but inevitable result was: nothing happened.

Nevertheless this development was unsettling. While I was happy at my work with the City Mission, the idea of exploring other spheres of Christian service lingered. A fresh face with a new vision might take the work forward in Ligoniel and Ballysillan. If I went elsewhere then I would be a fresh face to others. And yet, and yet ....

Two events - one sombre, one auspicious - straddled the approach from Ballymena. On 14th March 1954 the Ballysillan Congregation was cast into mourning by the unexpected death of Rev H V Clements. For seven months the congregation was vacant. Then on 14th October the auspicious event took place. The Rev Hugh Ivor Orr, who had been minister of Second Saintfield for five years, was installed as minister of Ballysillan.

Ivor Orr and I were born in the same year. (It is humbling to think that while he died in 1959 - a young man - here I am more than 40 years later writing about him.) We had more than our ages in common. We felt at ease with each other. Soon I was able to share with him the episode about Ballymena Congregational Church. He listened attentively.

Shortly afterwards, about 9.00 am on a Saturday in November I went into my study to make final preparations for my Sunday evening service. By midday when I went down for lunch I was at Wits' End Corner. Try as I might with texts and portions of Scripture I just could not get going. Like Hamlet when asked what he read, it was words, words, words. But the words would not fit together to make sense. My sermon would not come. Back into the study I went for the afternoon. I agonized over what my sermon would be. Nothing positive emerged. I was at an all-time low.

Next day being Sunday I was with the minister and some elders in the Session Room for prayer before the morning service. I went over to where Ivor Orr was standing at his desk to give him a message about someone who was sick. He caught my hand and said, 'Jackson, we were thinking about you all day yesterday. You should be thinking about going into the Church.'

It was hard to take in. A few hours earlier I had been at a standstill with sermon preparation, now it was being suggested that I should be considering the ministry - the Presbyterian ministry. When I was at my weakest God was speaking through the words of my friend, Ivor Orr. I do not think I am being sentimentally pious in thinking this way. After all God has,'*chosen the weak things of the world to confound the things which are mighty'* (1Cor 1:27).

During that particular Sunday morning service I confess that as I joined the congregation for worship I was doing little more than going through the motions. What Ivor Orr said would not go out of my mind. He was thinking of me all day yesterday .... I should be thinking of going into the church. He was thinking .... I should be thinking ......

For me it was a time of personal crisis in my spiritual pilgrimage. Never before nor since have I experienced anything quite like it. In sermon preparation I have had days of desperation as well as inspiration, but in no way have they compared with the utter bankruptcy of personal resources that I endured on that Saturday night in November 1954. It was as if God was bringing me to a recognition of my own brokenness so that I might realise how abundant and abounding his grace was, and is, and will continue to be.

The following Monday was another crucial day. As it happened, Ivor Orr and his wife, Ena, had arranged to meet us that night in order to get to know each other better. If Ivor and Ena really knew my background, or rather my lack of appropriate background for the Presbyterian ministry, would they still say I ought to think about it? The Orrs did not know that I had left school at fourteen, nor that I had not advanced myself educationally since I started work. I now told them. Far from saying - as many might understandably have done - that maybe the Church was not such a good idea after all, Ivor immediately undertook to teach me Latin and Greek.

Other questions forced themselves upon me. Even supposing I had the brains to master Latin and Greek and all the other subjects on the theological college curriculum would I have the stickability? Was it right to leave the Belfast City Mission where there had been so many encouragements? With a wife and son - Raymond was now seven years old - and without government or local authority grants or any significant savings what were we going to live on? Since 793 Crumlin Road was City Mission property, where would we live? Was it enough to drop down on our knees and trust that everything would just fall into place? Others in the City Mission had gone into the Church but were Daisy and I sure that this was God's will for me? Until near midnight we talked these matters over with the Orrs.

These then were three days in succession - Saturday, Sunday, Monday - that together were to change the course of my life. From that time on we decided to trust the Lord to open or close doors so that his leading might be clear.

Doors did begin to open and in very practical ways. For

the time being we stayed with the City Mission which meant we remained in 793 Crumlin Road Nearby was the Glenbank Bleach Works. From time to time engineers from England came to this firm to install or repair machinery. Glenbank approached us to see if we would take these men as lodgers. We agreed. As these engineers usually stayed for six months or a year we now had regular monthly cheques coming in so that our savings account began to grow.

Ivor Orr became my Latin tutor. Amo, amas, amat, amamus, amatus, amant - conjugation of Latin verbs and declension of Latin nouns were daunting concepts to me who had only a smattering of English grammar. But this was what was required for entrance to Magee University College on which I had now set my hopes. Had it not been for the patience and encouragement of Ivor, I am sure that I would have thrown the Latin textbook into the bin. Sometimes I felt that I myself was ready for binning.

I struggled on as best I could. Later I went to a private tutor but, because of my commitments as a missionary, studying was relegated to the hours between 11.00am and 2.00am. Physically, intellectual and emotionally I was being stretched. I asked the Lord to keep me in health and He did. Gradually other things began to fall into place and the way ahead became clearer.

By February 1956 I was ready to take the step of faith. I resigned from the Belfast City Mission. Out of 793 Crumlin Road we had to go. Back into 270 Ligoniel Road we went. Granny McKeown and Aunt Essie had already intimated their willingness to have us. Daisy, who had stopped work after the birth of Raymond, returned to business in Morgan's.

One problem arose from our flit. In No. 270 there was of course no space for our furniture. William J Morgan - the same man who had addressed the open-air - came to our rescue. His removal van and men arrived and took our bits and pieces into storage. We had no further sight of our furniture until we went to Newtownards in 1963 when again the Morgans did the necessaries. No bills ever had to be paid. The generosity of the Morgans was something to which, I am sure, others could also testify. We certainly experienced and appreciated it, not least because it came when we were most in need. What is more, it was done unobtrusively not, as is the manner of some, proclaimed from the rooftops.

With the practicalities attended to I was enrolled at Magee University College. I had to move away from wife and son and become a boarder at Magee. As I embarked on my Arts Course I had those feelings of apprehension that had troubled me before. But what hit me most was home sickness. How I missed Daisy and Raymond! For two weeks life was misery. Several times I was on the point of packing my bags and returning to Belfast. I cannot remember being able to share my feeling of utter loneliness with my fellow students; indeed I think this is the first time I have shared it with anyone.

Academic life has never been my forte. I am happier with people than with erudite tomes. So maybe because there is not a lot to tell I shall pass quickly over my scholastic career. Suffice it to say that I was permitted to take a shortened Arts Course which was accepted by the authorities at the Presbyterian College (Assembly's) in Belfast where I did enough, but probably not much more than that, to complete my theological and other courses. On 29th May 1962 I, along with seven fellow students, was licensed as a probationer for the ministry of the Presbyterian Church in Assembly's College Chapel.

During these years at Magee and Assembly's I did various jobs in the Summer and at Christmas. Two places of employment in particular I recall - the Dairy Department of the Cooperative on the Ravenhill Road and the Post Office. In Londonderry I acted as part-time assistant in Ebrington Presbyterian Church under the Rev James Sheppard Woods who also helped with the speech training of divinity students at Magee. He was a lovely gentleman from whom I learned much. And when that congregation sang:

Behold the mountain of the Lord
In latter days shall rise
On mountain tops above the hills,
And draw the wond'ring eyes. ....

it was an experience of being exalted above the humdrum of life into the very presence of God.

In Belfast my part-time assistantship was in Richview under the tutelage of the Rev David Porter. Like myself, he had served an apprenticeship in the Belfast City Mission. Before coming to Richview he ministered from 1931 until 1936 in Trinity, Ahoghill and from 1936 until 1946 in First Lurgan. I admired this man and his preaching so much that I found myself unconsciously adopting some of his mannerisms. Years later I was still raising myself on my toes while I preached just as David Porter had done.

Chapter 8

First notions and 2nd Newtownards

Having surprised myself by passing all the examinations required by the Board of Studies and succeeded in being licensed to preach the Gospel, I was ready for the next step in my progress. Over the years the procedures have changed, but in the Sixties there had to be an interval of at least six months between licensing and ordination. Now at the age of 41, I was eligible for a call to a congregation.

At this important stage in my life I wondered where God would lead me. I suppose that with my 'country' upbringing my natural inclination was to favour a rural church but on the other hand, from 1944 my Christian work had been carried out in an urban environment. How was I to know the will of God?

Towards the end of 1962 and the opening months of 1963

five or six congregations approached me. As a result my name was put on two lists. For a variety of reasons I withdrew from one of these lists. The other congregation called one of my colleagues. Within a few weeks I had both turned, and been turned, down.

As time passed, the vacant congregations were getting what is called fixed up while I remained unfixed. Two congregations, still without ministers, caught my eye. One was Second Newtownards. The other was a rural congregation also in County Down. I felt I should apply for both, trusting God to engineer the circumstances so that I could find the place of His choice. As I posted both applications into the very same letterbox I remember asking myself, 'Will I take the first positive approach - wherever it comes from - as an indication of God's leading?'

Honesty compels me to admit that I was longing in my heart of hearts that the rural congregation would be the first to meet to make a call. If that congregation did not show an interest in me, then I would be happy to go to Second Newtownards - provided of course that the people there would have me! The sequence of events did not work out quite as I would have liked. On Sunday, 5th May, 1963 I preached at both services in Second Newtownards. Two weeks later I took my turn in the list of the rural congregation.

The convener of the 'country' vacancy had invited me for lunch. As we sat around the table chatting he somewhat startled me by saying, 'Jackson, you are only wasting your time preaching here. Tomorrow night the Second Newtownards congregation is meeting to make out a call. I was in Ards yesterday and you are going to get the call.'

'I wouldn't be so sure,' I replied.

That Sunday evening I returned home very favourably

impressed with the whole set-up in the rural congregation. As I was thinking along these lines the phone rang. It was one of my best friends, one who knew both congregations very well.

'You have done well today,' he began. ''So well,' he continued, ''that I believe that you will receive the call from this church when they meet in two weeks' time.' He concluded by advising me to withdraw from the Second Newtownard's list.

Though this was in one sense music to my ears in another sense it was discomfiting. Having embarked on a course of action I felt bound to proceed. My response to my friend had to be, 'No, I cannot do that.' But in the back of my mind I would probably have been happy at the thought of Second Newtownards rejecting me.

The next twenty-four hours were a time of waiting. Then late on the evening of 20th May the phone rang again. This time it was the Rev C H McKeown, minister of Regent Street and convener of the Newtownards' vacancy. At their meeting the congregation had issued a call to me. 'It was not,' said Mr McKeown, 'a unanimous call, but you did get two-thirds of the votes cast. Will you accept?'

At that time - and indeed at other times - many ministers stipulated that they would only accept a call if it was unanimous. I had made no such stipulation. I accepted the call. On 27th June 1963 I was ordained and installed as minister of Second Newtownards. In early September Daisy, Raymond (now 16 years old) and I moved into the manse.

Second Newtownards was an old established congregation, having started - without a building - in the mid-18th century as an Anti-burgher Seceder congregation. I was the ninth minister. My immediate predecessor, the Rev Samuel Thomas Palmer, had ministered to the people of Newtownards for 23 years and had a new hall named after him. He died on 7

January, 1963. When I became minister the congregation consisted of 245 families representing 820 persons of whom 154 were communicants with 10 elders, and 122 children on the Sabbath School and Bible Class rolls.

Although I had not received a unanimous call, we as a family were made very welcome by members of the congregation, also by neighbours and citizens of the Borough of Ards. On visiting I was well received. But one of my early calls is still vivid in my mind. The man of the house said to me, 'I suppose you have heard about me?'

'No, what do you mean?' I asked.

'Well,' he retorted, 'I didn't vote for you and I refused to sign your call.'

'I won't hold that against you.' I replied, 'You probably voted for the right man, but I'm sorry, you'll just have to put up with me.'

Far from driving a wedge between us his Ulster bluntness was the beginning of a firm friendship. That man became one of my most faithful supporters in the work of the Kingdom. When I left just more than seven years later, he said that no one could have done more for the congregation than Jackson Buick.

Visiting was something I enjoyed - much more so than the lecture theatre or examination room. I felt privileged to be involved with people in the work of the Kingdom. By sharing in their joys and sorrows, hopes and disappointments I was drawn closer to them. As in most congregations some families suffered tragic and sudden death. Often these trying experiences were faced with a fortitude and serenity that bore witness to the grace and love of God.

Preaching I also enjoyed. Each Sunday there were two services. Attendances were most encouraging and increased with the passing years. Seven years into my ministry a deputation from Craigy Hill in Larne came to hear me. Although it was an ordinary Sunday morning service the church was packed to the door. This turned out to be a significant day which was to have personal repercussions, so it is something to which I shall return.

One of the reasons for the influx into the congregation was the movement of people from the Lower Ards Peninsula into the town of Ards. By 1970 when I moved on, the congregation had grown to 350 families consisting of 1110 persons, 220 of whom were communicants, 11 elders and 190 children on the rolls of the Sabbath Schools and Bible Classes. To the Youth organisations already in existence - the Girls' Brigade and Youth Club - were added the Boys' Brigade and Christian Endeavour with a thriving Junior Section.

Several missions were held. The first was conducted by the Rev James Leonard Heaney who had served in Hill Street, Lurgan before coming to Mountpottinger in 1962. The attendance was heartening and this mission proved a time of blessing.

In 1967 the Rev Arthur Malcolm Parke, whose father and one of whose brothers were also Presbyterian ministers (another being a medical missionary in China), led a week of Bible studies. Unlike his father whose ministry was cut short by an early motor accident in 1919, Malcolm Parke had a long ministry - from 1941 until 1975 - in Orangefield. His teaching proved to be a time of edification and refreshment for the whole church.

In 1970 the five Presbyterian churches in Newtownards united for an outreach to the entire Borough. Over a 4-6 week period each church planned a series of Sunday services on agreed topics. This was followed by a further week of evangelistic meetings, each church picking their own evangelist. In Second Newtownards the man chosen was the

Rev Alan Flavelle who at that time was the minister of Mourne and later moved to Finaghy.

In the Summer of 1970 another form of outreach was tried. Using the Town Square we organised a Drive-in Church which attracted a sizeable crowd. Most of the people simply sat in their cars parked in the Square and listened to the message. The Ards Council was kind enough to allow us to plug our amplification system into their office supply. Over the four Sunday evenings interest increased. At the last meeting at the end of August there were many requests for a return to the Square in 1971 but by then I had moved to Larne.

As I reflect on those years in Newtownards I am conscious of how happy they were. Of course there were problems and even crises but in coping with these I became, I hope, more mature. While the years in the Belfast City Mission and then in Assembly's College had given me experience in certain situations, working as a minister in the Presbyterian Church was quite another matter. But in time the rough edges were smoothed - at least some of them - and I realized that I had still had much to learn. Even at eighty years of age I am still learning.

Presbyterians are noted for their emphasis on individual conscience. In turn this can lead to great diversity of opinion in, say, Session and Committee. In Second Newtownards differences arose not so much from the theological as from the administrative and organisational perspective. There is always the danger of discussion degenerating into a tug-of-war between personalities rather than concentrating on principles. For the smooth, effective work of the church patience, sensitivity, understanding and graciousness are required from all. In Session and Committee the benediction should be the conclusion, not the start, of business.

Humour is another useful quality. And thank goodness

The Kirk Session in Second Newtownards

all Presbyterians are not po-faced. In Second Newtownards Johnny Pagan - a misnomer of a surname, if ever there was one - often brought a smile to faces and lightened our footsteps. Johnny was a highly respected elder with a nimble wit. When church attendance started to increase Johnny nicknamed me 'The Ferret.' Then when I got involved in missions and preaching engagements elsewhere he described me as 'a half-time minister.'

I remember one summer evening being told that one of the leading evangelists (and future Moderator) of the Presbyterian Church was to attend our evening service. I admit being uneasy with the presence of any ministerial colleagues - I do not relish preaching to preachers - and here was a prince of preachers. When I joined the choir for a pre-service prayer I said, 'Sing as you have never sung before, for one of our church's leading preachers is here tonight.' To this Johnny made a remark which I did not quite catch. 'What's that he said?' I asked. 'After tonight he'll know there is another,' was another choir member's repeat of Johnny's remark.

This little comment released my tension and throughout the service I felt quite at ease.

Chapter 9

Old and New

In 1961 Second Newtownards had ordained seven elders; towards the end of my ministry eight more were added. The office bearers who welcomed me were George Newell, Clerk of Session, Harry Beale, Treasurer and John Algie, secretary. John had the honour of being twice Mayor of the Borough. Sadly George Newell died suddenly. A memorial minute in the Session Book of September 1964 pays tribute to his long years of Christian service in the congregation. Harry Beale now became Clerk of Session and George Ferguson was appointed Treasurer.

Three of the young elders ordained on 21st June 1970 went on into what is often called 'full-time service' though, I suppose, when you think of it, for Christians there should be no such thing as part-time service. Be that as it may, George Ferguson is now Executive Secretary of the Belfast City Mission. Roy Graham took up work with the Child Evangelism Fellowship, then became a Baptist pastor serving for a short time in Craigavon. Hastings McIntyre has recently become the minister of Cregagh Presbyterian Church, having served previously in Castlereagh. Another person from Second Newtownards to go into (yes, that term again) 'full-time service' was Freda Algie. At present she is the headmistress of the Wives' School in Zomba Theological College in Malawi. For a short period before her departure she served as Woman Worker in her home congregation

By 17th June 1970 - that is after seven years - Daisy and I felt that we were no longer considered as imports into the Borough. Our roots were deepening. Our knowledge of the place was increasing. Ards itself was a fine shopping town, convenient to the coast and Belfast. It was a thriving, industrious place with, it seemed, a good future. All in all it was a pleasant location in which to live.

As for the congregation in which I ministered it was a comfortable enough size for me to manage - big enough to be a full-time ministry, small enough to retain a sense of intimacy. In the will of God Daisy and I would have been happy to continue in Newtownards and complete a lengthy ministry (though hardly as long as the 47 years of my 19th century predecessor, Rev David Maxwell.)

Still, no matter how contented we felt, we also knew that if we were to follow the One who said, '*I will make you fishers of men,*' we might be called upon to cast our nets in other fishing grounds.

As it happened, I had become involved in the Girls' Brigade not only at local, but also as a member of the N. Ireland Divisional Board, at provincial level. In 1970 my responsibility was the setting of the annual Scripture examination. The chairman of the Board was the Rev R V A (Victor) Lynas who, in 1972 became Moderator and was awarded a DD degree. In 1970 he had been the minister of Gardenmore Presbyterian Church in Larne for 23 years. In the same year he was also the convener of a vacancy in Craigy Hill congregation, situated in a new housing development to the northwest of Gardenmore.

Because of our common interest in Girls' Brigade, Victor Lynas and I were in occasional contact with each other. During one of these contacts - it must have been about the end of August 1970 - he asked me, almost casually, if I ever thought of a move. I replied that I was encouraged by, and contented in, the work in Second Newtownards. Then jokingly I added, 'However if Fisherwick called me I would have to think about it!'

Two weeks later we were in touch again, this time by phone. The business was still to do with the Girls' Brigade. Before Victor Lynas rang off, he came back in a specific way to what he had touched on generally before.

'Are you preaching in your own church on Sunday week - that is the second Sunday in September?' he asked. He went on to say, 'Your name has been mentioned in connection with a vacancy in Craigy Hill. The Session there is talking about coming to hear you.' To put it mildly this was totally unexpected but Mr Lynas had put it over in such a matter-of-fact way that I do not think I was as surprised as I should have been.

In the third weekend in September 1970 I had to go to Ballymena to attend the Convention of the Irish CE Union of which I was a council member. On my return journey I suddenly remembered what Victor Lynas had said. When I arrived home about 11 o'clock on Saturday night there was a message for me. I was to go to the home of one of my church members. It was past midnight before I got sitting down to look over my sermon notes and make final preparations for the service of the same day.

Soon the clock's hands were pointing to 11.30 am. The church was packed out, even the gallery. Like other ministers I have conducted services when, despite careful preparation, everything has gone wrong. On this autumnal Sunday morning everything went right. If I had started with the benediction and done the service in reverse I feel everything would still have gone well. Looking down from the pulpit I spied strangers in the house - not as in parliament unauthorised, but from, and approved by, the Craigy Hill Kirk Session.

At the close of the service I went as usual to the door to shake hands with the departing worshippers. Curiously I do not recall meeting, never mind speaking to, the strangers. If I remember correctly, I did have a phone call during that Sunday afternoon. Someone - I do not know who - wanted to know if I was preaching in Glengormley that evening. My answer was in the affirmative for I was involved with the well-known evangelist, Michael Perrott, in a series of meetings in that congregation. In subsequent days I often wondered if that phone call was from a member in Craigy Hill and if he turned up in Glengormley.

As September ebbed away I was working at preparation for the Winter session. I was finding it most difficult. I would work at trying to get something down on paper only to discard it. This happened over and over again. I also remember thinking to myself, 'You are not going to Craigy Hill.'

The same message was being delivered to me indirectly by a church member whom I had been visiting over several weeks in the Belfast City Hospital. He was one of those men - there are still some of them around - who seem to know everything that is happening in every vacancy. During one of my visits he raised the topic of Craigy Hill.

'I understand that Craigy Hill is planning to go out and

hear more men,' he said. I listened. What else could I do? The weeks were passing, nothing was happening. I was beginning to deduce that when Craigy Hill made out their call it would not be to me.

On the fourth Sunday evening in October I was sitting in the manse with my friend, David Johnston, when the phone rang. A voice said, ' Jackson, this is Victor. The Craigy Hill hearing committee met tonight. I am ringing to tell you that they have unanimously decided to put your name as the sole nominee to a congregational meeting on 6 November. Will you allow your name to go forward?'

Watching me take this call, David Johnston said my face changed colour. Much more was to change over the next few weeks. But for the moment I was caught somewhat off balance. 'I'll need time to think and pray about this,' I responded, 'and to talk it over with Daisy.'

Victor Lynas readily agreed, assuring me that if I felt I needed his help he was available. I must have contacted him on the Monday morning for it was arranged that we would meet on Tuesday afternoon at Craigy Hill. Victor Lynas and his wife, Margaret, showed Daisy and me through the church, hall and manse. We finished by having tea in the Gardenmore Manse. It had been a pleasant visit, profitable too. Yet to me things were not crystal clear.

On Wednesday my former boss, the Rev David Porter (by now retired) and his wife Lena, invited us for lunch. For hours our conversation centred on the interest of, and possible call to, Craigy Hill. After lunch David and I went for a long walk where the pros and cons of Craigy Hill were gone over in some detail. Later, as the Porters were leaving, David turned to me and said, 'You know that Lena and I will be praying over the next few days.'

On Thursday morning Daisy and I decided to put Craigy

Hill aside at least till evening. Daisy got on with her household chores. I went out on home and hospital visitation, catching up on the routine work of the ministry. Then about 9.00 pm we sat down beside the fire to relax and have supper. In depth Daisy and I went over, yet again, the points for and against moving to Craigy Hill. Should we walk away from Second Newtownards where God was blessing the work? On the other hand there seemed no good reason why we should not leave ourselves in God's hands as far as Craigy Hill was concerned. Since God's call comes through His people this meant leaving the matter to the Larne congregation trusting that as they prayed they would be led aright. If the Craigy Hill Church issued a call to me my response would be positive.

Friday morning came. We had our breakfast and devotions. While our minds had not changed from the previous evening, I decided to delay contacting the Craigy Hill convener until midday. At noon Daisy and I had another short chat and probably a prayer. I dialled the Gardenmore number. I told Victor Lynas that if the Craigy Hill congregation did call me I would respond positively. 'But,' I continued, 'I am glad that I myself do not have the final decision to make.'

About one hour later - as we were having lunch - the phone rang. The voice at the other end said, 'This is George Gillespie, the Clerk of Session of Craigy Hill. Mr Lynas has just told me that you are allowing your name to be put before the congregation on 6th November. I am very delighted.' These words did something for Daisy and me. In a way they signalled the nature of the relationships that were to develop in the years ahead.

The congregational meeting was - I learnt afterwards - happy and harmonious, closing with the singing of the doxology. This time the call was unanimous. I took this to be the indication of God's will for me. I accepted the call.

When the call was being presented to the Ards Presbytery, the Rev Lynas revealed something about my career that even I had not been aware of. Back in 1963 when Craigy Hill was still a Church Extension Charge - and vacant - my name had been under consideration. At that time the Mission Board had issued the call to the Rev William Brown. Victor Lynas suggested - perhaps in jest - that I had not made it then simply because BR comes before BU alphabetically!

My Installation was held on Thursday 17 December. The Service was conducted by the Moderator of the Carrickfergus Presbytery, the Rev R G Craig (First Carrickfergus) with the charge to minister and people being given by the Rev C F Young (Ballylinney). On the following Sunday - a few days before Christmas - I mounted the Craigy Hill pulpit for the first time.

The congregation in Larne was quite a contrast to the one in Newtownards. Second Newtownards was more than two centuries old; Craigy Hill was less than two decades old. The former had a well-established congregation with about 100 senior citizens; the latter was seething with young life. Indeed Craigy Hill was known as the Children's Church for it had been built in the mid-1950s from the contributions of children and young people in the Presbyterian Church throughout Ireland. By 1970 I had become the fourth minister in this congregation's 14-year history. The Revs Bill Boyd, William Brown and James Fullerton had all come and gone. In Second Newtownards I had been the fourth minister in the previous 102 years which of course represented less than half its history. Moving from the old and settled, to the new and unsettled, was to keep me on my toes.

CHAPTER 10

CRAIGY HILL AND BRUSTIN BRAE

In Craigy Hill, Daisy and I soon settled into our new home. The manse, just recently built, was on the Brustin Brae Road. It commanded - more particularly in summer - a stunning view across the North Channel to the hills of Scotland. In Winter the retribution was exacted by the buffeting from the westerly gales. Not far away were the hills of County Antrim: Shane's Hill (over which one passed on the way to Ballymena), Agnew's Hill (North of this) and Sallagh Braes (a favourite place for walks and picnics). The roads up from the town of Larne - the Roddens, Lower Cairncastle Road and Mill Brae - were steep enough to require a gear change before reaching the new housing estates of Antiville and Craigy Hill.

The Craigy Hill Church had been opened by the then Moderator of the General Assembly, the Rt Rev A A Fulton PhD

DD, on 11th March 1961. It had been built strategically on the Churchill Road right between the Borough Council estate of Antiville and the Housing Trust estate of Craigy Hill. On the other side of the Churchill Road was a fine church hall. Under a reconstruction programme the Getty Mission Hall in Larne had been demolished, and since part of the funding for the new hall had come from the Getty Trust, the new hall was called the Getty Memorial Hall. It had been opened on 18 November 1966.

As we accustomed ourselves to our new surroundings, I reflected on just how wonderfully blessed we were by the warmth and sincerity of our welcome. All along we had that comforting feeling of being really wanted. Maybe this had something to do with the fact that my immediate predecessor had stayed only 18 months. I remember quipping that Second Newtownards had buried my predecessor and I got out alive, and that Craigy Hill had chased my predecessor but that they might be carrying me out on their shoulders. As to whether they now wished me a long or short life I was discreet enough not to inquire. Anyhow when I left Craigy Hill $11^{1/2}$ years later, it was by the downward road which joined the A8 for Belfast, not the upward road which led to the Larne cemetery.

In 1970 statistics show that Craigy Hill consisted of 515 families with 680 FWO contributors and 264 communicants. But the really challenging figure was the 483 children on the rolls of the Sunday Schools and Bible Classes. Leadership here was in the hands of Crawford Adair, Tom Ringland and Mrs Harrison. Joan Dundee and William Simms were captains of the Girls' and Boys' Brigades respectively. George Gillespie was Clerk of Session, Bob Ferguson Secretary, and Arthur Henderson Treasurer. And who was the organist? None other than Beth Porter, the very woman, who 33 years previously at a bus stop in Antrim, had challenged me about my faith.

As I think back on the office bearers and staff in the organisations and indeed, in some cases their successors, I am still struck by the dedication and vision of so many. Leadership was so competent that, while I was kept informed of what was happening or going to happen, I did not have to spend time running around to see if everything was progressing satisfactorily.

The efficient running of church affairs left me free to carry on my pastoral and preaching responsibilities without having to worry about organisations being in fact disorganised. For this I was thankful. On the other hand it left me with no excuse for getting on with the other work to be done. The Rev James Fullerton had set a cracking pace in visitation by getting around the congregation twice in his short ministry. Even with the priority I put on visiting homes and hospitals and my love for it, this was an achievement I could not hope to emulate.

It was against a background such as I have outlined that I took up my work as the minister of Craigy Hill. Often in my prayers - public and private - I used the words of the psalmist, *'The lines are fallen unto me in pleasant places; yea, I have a goodly heritage'* (Ps 16:6). In truth I was of the opinion that Craigy Hill was one of those pleasant places.

From my $11^{1/2}$ years in Larne it is possible to pick out only a few of the episodes and incidents for fuller treatment. One issue that came to the fore in the 1970s was the Presbyterian Church's membership of the World Council of Churches. Increasingly members in the pew were becoming uneasy about where the WCC was heading. Its theology, insofar as it had any, seemed liberationist in the political sense rather in the evangelical sense of setting man free from the bondage of sin.

Sometimes there was a lack of judgement or at the very least the pursuit of a line of action that inevitably led to controversy. In Africa a grant of $85,000 from the WCC's Special Fund to the Rhodesian Patriotic Front sat uneasily with the murder of six Elim pastors.

Inside Presbyterianism a group began to appeal to the Church to sever its links with the WCC. By reversing these initials to CCW to stand for the Campaign for Complete Withdrawal, this group - mainly evangelical - gradually built up support for its cause, not least among the eldership.

I think we in Craigy Hill were one of the few sessions to accept the invitation from Church House to submit our views on the WCC. The Clerk of Session prepared a 3,000 word document which highlighted the concerns of ourselves and others. Three main criticisms were put forward. The WCC offered (1) compromise rather than Christianity, (2) an ethical programme rather than an evangelical outreach, and (3) a Romish stance rather than a Reformation stand. Attention was drawn to the second of John Cogley's Ten Commandments for the Ecumenical Age: 'Do not look to conversion as the proper result of ecumenism.' This seemed to summarise WCC thinking. In short the ecumenist preferred to share insights rather than win converts, except of course to ecumenism.

For several years the debates in the General Assembly were quite heated and attracted a lot of public attention. Bob Ferguson, Craigy Hill's representative elder, joined a delegation which included the Very Rev Dr A J Weir, Rev Douglas Armstrong, Rev W M Craig, Rev K N E Newell and W J McWilliam. Their task was to meet WCC representatives and urge upon them, 'the deep concern felt in our Church, particularly over the issues raised by the Special Fund.' By 1980 the arguments against continuing WCC membership prevailed;

by a majority of 60 (448 to 388) the General Assembly agreed to withdraw from the World Council of Churches.

In the aftermath of the Feakle talks (1974) - cloaked in mystery and unproductive of any termination of violence - the Craigy Hill Session also met representatives of the Government Committee under the Moderator, the Rt Rev Dr Temple Lundie. That novices from a new congregation should have such ready access to Church headquarters was a tribute to the democratic structures of Presbyterianism. Less satisfactory was the outcome for, after almost two hours, it was not clear who had put who right.

One project with which the Craigy Hill Session was able to identify enthusiastically was Flame '74. The aim was 'to devise practical ways of inspiring and enabling ordinary members of the Church to accept their responsibilities in the sphere of outreach and Christian witnesses'. Bob Ferguson was appointed to head a publicity committee and Muriel McCabe - a lady involved in many aspects of church work - acted as press officer. Flame '74 was divided into three phases.

Phase I was a call to personal commitment from the communicant membership. Prayer was a priority. The congregation was encouraged to plead with God for a movement of his Holy Spirit.

In Phase II the stress was on training so that people could witness to their faith in everyday life. One feature was the arrangement of Guest Services which were followed by a cup of tea. In the week leading up to Easter meetings were addressed by invited speakers. For instance the Rev Harry Uprichard of Trinity, Ahoghill, spoke on the Resurrection and the Second Coming.

In September Phase III started with a mission conducted by the Rev Eric Gardner of First Ballymena. In the run-up to the meetings the elders and other helpers from Craigy Hill received additional support from an Irish Mission team consisting of Tom Hollywood and Espie Young. The Superintendent, the Rev Jim Hagan, also paid us a visit. We were encouraged and strengthened by Eric Gardiner's ministry. A few who seldom appeared at public worship did respond, but the meetings - as so often happens - were supported mainly by church going people. Phase III was supposed to stretch into the years ahead. As one of the Flame '74 leaflets put it: 'There is no end in sight, for God's commands span the years ..'

Seven years later Craigy Hill reached its Silver Jubilee. In September 1981 past ministers and assistants conducted worship. Then on Sunday, 4th October, the Rev John Maddock of Carryduff started an anniversary mission. Attendance was rather disappointing but God did move by his Spirit. Several young women were converted, to be followed at a later date by their husbands.

Blessing was also experienced among the young. At Boys' Brigade Summer Camps - with Robert Webb now captain - several boys came to faith in Christ. One boy - Bobby Liddle - went into the ministry and is now the minister of Legacurry Presbyterian Church. In those days as an active Boys' Brigader he brought an elderly disabled member in a wheelchair to church each Sunday.

As I have indicated, it is possible to record only a small - a very small - fraction of my life in Craigy Hill or indeed elsewhere. There are however a few more matters on which I would like to comment.

Already it will be obvious that the Session was very active and, in debate, forthright and honest. When problems did occur they were not evaded. Elders were neither 'Yes minister' nor 'No minister' men. Two men might come into a meeting together, take the opposite sides in some debate, and after the benediction leave together still the best of friends.

If forthrightness was in danger of exceeding its limits, someone would utter a cautionary word. In one tense meeting I remember an elder - I think it was Charles Meban - saying, 'Moderator, I believe we should all think carefully before we speak.'

One other night when, I suppose, I had been pontificating on some subject Graham Gaston said, 'Moderator, we are all right behind you.' To this Arthur Henderson responded, 'Yes, but we are so far behind him that he doesn't know we are there.'

With Arthur also in charge of church finances committee meetings ran smoothly. But here, too, the serious items on the agenda could be interspersed with humour. Some committee members needed lifts. Each committee night Bob Morrow, now deceased, called for Muriel McCabe who had - and still has - an ebullient personality but never married. On this particular night I noticed Bob Morrow sitting in the meeting but no Muriel McCabe.

'Where is Muriel tonight?' I asked. 'Ooooooh!' exclaimed Bob darting out of the room like lightning.

By the time he returned - with Muriel - the meeting had started. As Muriel walked across the room to her usual seat she said in a loud, clear voice, 'As usual men have let me down.'

The gathering collapsed in laughter. I need hardly add that people like Muriel McCabe and Bob Morrow were the heart and soul of the place.

During my time in Craigy Hill I had two summer assistants. This was appreciated as the congregation was increasing in size. The first summer assistant was Ian McNie who, like Daisy and myself, had been brought up in the First Antrim Congregation. For three summers Ian laboured with us, much loved and greatly appreciated by the people. Noth-

CRAIGY HILL 25TH ANNIVERSARY 1981

SESSION & COMMITTEE WITH THE MODERATOR OF THE GENERAL ASSEMBLY
THE RT REV DR JOHN GIRVAN

ing was too much trouble for him. He would beg, borrow but just stop short of stealing to help a lame dog over a style.

Craigy Hill was greatly indebted to Ian McNie, but as it turned out Ian McNie was greatly indebted to Craigy Hill, for it was from among the members of the congregation that he made the discovery of Proverbs 18:22: '*Whoso findeth a wife findeth a good thing, and obtaineth favour from the Lord.*' Her name was Anne Thompson. One of the finest young ladies in the district, Anne was to manifest her many gifts of heart, hand and mind in the years ahead.

After leaving Craigy Hill Ian McNie went to Alexandra to be assistant with the Rev Martin Smyth, later to become Unionist MP for South Belfast. From there Ian proceeded to be Minister of Kilkeel, then of Trinity in Ballymoney.

Chapter 11

Pulpit and Prison

In some autobiographies Christian pastors recount - often in dramatic terms - how, by the grace of God, they graduated from prison to pulpit. My story goes in the opposite direction. I went from pulpit - in Craigy Hill - to prison - in Crumlin Road. How, why and for what conviction will be revealed in this chapter.

But before my time in prison there is more to tell about my days in Larne. With the departure of Ian McNie there was going to be a gap, especially in work with the young. Fortunately we were able to acquire more help very quickly. David Johnston became our second summer assistant. He proved to be an excellent worker sharing eagerly and thoughtfully in the pastoral and preaching responsibilities.

Like Ian McNie, David Johnston had as one of his main tasks the organisation of the yearly CSSM programme. One of the helpers was a lovely, copper-headed girl called Olive.

She was an outstanding leader of young people. A romance developed. Eventually - and perhaps inevitably - Olive became Mrs Johnston. But unlike his predecessor's romance, David's was only indirectly linked to Larne for both he and Olive belonged to Coleraine.

David Johnston was - and, I suppose, still is - a talented pianist. Even as an assistant he was a challenging preacher. He also knew his own mind. At a time when Bible translations could generate controversy he caused a mild stir by reading from the Revised Standard Version. At a Session meeting shortly afterwards the Craigy Hill elders had a lively, well-tempered, enjoyable and worthwhile debate on the merits and demerits of various versions of the Bible.

From Craigy Hill David Johnston moved on to be ordained assistant in Mourne Presbyterian Church. In 1983 he was installed in Waringstown and Bellville, then in 1994 in Hamilton Road, Bangor.

Craigy Hill's first full-time assistant was Hugh Robert Quinn. He was ordained in January 1981 and with his wife, Helen, and children, Philip, Deborah and Jalon served in Larne for a short but significant period. In a congregation where there were so many young families the fact that they had three children - a fourth, Esther, was born later - did no harm at all. Already Robin, as he was known, and Helen had a wealth of gifts and experience for they had served as missionaries in Uganda where there was poverty. Now their missionary talents were brought to bear in a part of the world where there was growing affluence.

Robin and I worked together as equals, our strengths complimenting each other. We cooperated as friends rather than as master and pupil. Each week we met to pray together and plan the week ahead. Every three months we prepared a preaching plan - something that is essential where two or more share the ministry, otherwise the spiritual food is likely to lack essential nutrients. Robin also took his full part in the administration of the sacraments, visitation, funerals and the like. Indeed I look back upon those days as among the happiest of my ministry. In every way I found Robin to be an excellent colleague.

But the siren call of Africa was still sounding in the Quinns' ears. After a commissioning service in February 1982 they left Northern Ireland to take up work in Zomba Theological College in Malawi. This event had an inhibiting but not terminal effect upon what was beginning to brew in my mind.

As a result of the untimely death of the Rev William Vance an advertisement appeared in the Presbyterian Herald indicating that there was likely to be a vacancy for a chaplain in Crumlin Road Prison. A similar position was probably going to be in need of filling at the Maze Prison. During the 1970s I had been making periodic visits to both these institutions. More than once my mind began to dwell on the great need I felt existed. If an opportunity arose - I thought - would I do something about it? At that time the convener of the Assembly's Chaplains' Committee was the Rev Harold Allen, minister of Ballyclare Presbyterian Church. As a fellow presbyter and friend I had several unofficial conversations with him about these vacancies.

By now I had been in Craigy Hill for eleven years. Somehow I considered I was not making the impact I would have liked. On the other hand I was sensing the tug of prison chaplaincy. It would be challenging - and different - work but, as I thought, prayed and talked the matter over with friends, it became more appealing.

Upon speaking yet again to Harold Allen, he urged me to allow my name to go forward so that it could be considered at the February meeting of the General Board. My response was hesitant.

'Look, Harold,' I said, 'Craigy Hill is already losing their assistant. I just cannot allow my name to go forward - no, not in February. Maybe I will consider it for the April Board meeting.'

The next thing I knew was that Harold Allen had arranged for the Interviewing Panel to meet in early March. 'Jackson,' he said, 'I want you to be at that interview.'

Others used their powers of persuasion. In particular the Rt Rev Dr John Girvan of Hill Street, Lurgan who was the current Moderator and the Rev Harry Allen of New Row, Coleraine, who was to become Moderator in 1996, urged me to let my name go forward for the Crumlin Road vacancy. For me this was the setting of the cat among the pigeons.

I decided to consult with the Craigy Hill office-bearers whom I invited to the manse on the Thursday night before the Monday morning interview. This Cabinet of the Church, as I liked to think of them, consisted of the Clerk of Session, Bob Ferguson, the Secretary, Bob McCann, and the Treasurer, Arthur Henderson. For a variety of reasons I also included George Gillespie who had, until recently, been Clerk of Session. With this group I shared my problem. I was looking to see if convincing reasons might be put as to why I should withdraw my name, for Daisy and I were still very happy in Craigy Hill.

Together we decided we would pray and think about the matter over the next few days. Then on the Sunday night George Gillespie was to have a chat with me. This took place alright but all things considered I concluded that I should attend the interview the next morning.

On Monday morning I set off for Belfast. I turned up for the interview happy to accept the decision of the Interview

Panel as God's guidance for my future. The Rt Rev Dr John Girvan was in the chair. During the interview I felt quite relaxed. Sitting there in what was supposed to be the hot seat I do not remember any fiery questions or simmering uneasiness.

About lunchtime Daisy and I returned to Larne. Having had something to eat I set out, as was my custom, to do some visits. Shortly after 5.00 PM I returned, again as was my custom, for an evening meal.

'You may pack your bags!' was Daisy's greeting. 'Harold Allen called earlier in the afternoon to inform you that you had been appointed Chaplain at Crumlin Road Prison and at the Hydebank Young Offenders' Centre.'

God had convicted me by his Holy Spirit acting through his Body, the Church, of where I ought to be. I was on the brink of a new life.

'If you are appointed to the Chaplaincy,' the Very Rev Dr Jack Weir had said at the interview, 'one of your jobs will be to educate the Church about this section of society.'

Whether I have succeeded in this, I am not sure. What I do know is that I have addressed about 240 meetings - PWA and Men's Groups, Church congregations and various other gatherings.

In March 1982 all this lay far in the distance. In the next few chapters I recount some experiences of my years in prison.

Chapter 12

Crumlin Road and Hydebank

On 2nd June 1982 I was installed as the prison chaplain for Her Majesty's Prison, commonly known as Crumlin Road, and the Young Offenders' Centre at Hydebank Wood. As I took my vows in Crumlin Road Presbyterian Church, I had mixed feelings. Here was a completely new area of Christian service - how would I cope?

Apprehensive as I was, a colleague must have been much more so. He was told only on a Monday morning that he was expected to take up his chaplaincy the following Sunday. No thinking time, no planning time, no preparatory course - he was transferred to his new post, it might be said, without undue delay. As for myself, I had two months in which to think about my new post - two months to get used to the idea in my mind. Then four months into my work I was sent to Wakehurst

Prison College in England for a week's training.

Once I got involved with the prisoners I discovered just how dissimilar the work was from what I had been doing as a minister of a congregation. Even the preaching and pastoral aspects had significant differences. For instance, in Crumlin Road the preaching was shared on a rota with the Rev David Jardine (Church of Ireland) and the Rev Robert Russell (Methodist). In Hydebank I alternated with the Rev Robert Bell (Church of Ireland) and the Rev Ken Wilson (Methodist). We met to co-ordinate our preaching programmes. My responsibility was for a service every other week in Crumlin Road and every third week in Hydebank.

At Crumlin Road services numbers fluctuated between 60 and 100; at Hydebank between 35 and 55. Contrary to popular opinion, attendance is not obligatory; prisoners had to indicate that they wanted to attend. Occasionally a prisoner complained that an officer had forgotten to unlock their cell door thus preventing him from going to worship. As a precaution, and in order to forestall trouble, prisoners were brought along in groups of about ten. It took about fifteen minutes to ensure that all had arrived.

Prisoners from different wings of the jail were seated apart from each other but they could - and did - talk over to each other. Sometimes a prisoner would move across the aisle and slip a note or maybe snout (tobacco) to a mate from another wing.

It hardly needs to be said that many men did not come to the services out of the highest spiritual motive. At a basic level it represented an hour out of the cell. The time - not least the ten minutes before the start of the service - afforded an opportunity to socialise, maybe to meet a mate from another wing. But when the service started the talking stopped. While the atmosphere was not quite that of Second Newtownards or

Craigy Hill there was a sense of reverence and the men were under the sound of the gospel. The presence of Christian prisoners was always an asset.

In my early days in Crumlin Road one such Christian was a prisoner called David Hamilton. Because of his deep tan complexion David went by the perhaps politically incorrect nickname of Paki or Packie. Over the years he bore a consistent witness, respected by both staff and inmates. He had a beautiful singing voice. At the services he and other Christian prisoners sat in the front seat. They were as good as - and maybe better than - many a church choir.

After release Paki worked as an evangelist with Prison Fellowship (Northern Ireland). Indeed he was the first ex-prisoner to receive clearance from the Northern Ireland Office to visit prisons in this capacity. For a further ten years he worked with Teen Challenge. More recently he has been working as a freelance international evangelist with the world as his parish.

It was Paki that reminded me of something that had gone completely out of my head. Apparently on the first Sunday that I took the service in Crumlin Road I took up a position behind the reading desk. According to Paki my first words were, 'Will I preach over this or under it?' 'That broke the ice,' said Paki, 'and from then on you were accepted by the prisoners.' Upon such simple incidents whole relationships can be made or broken.

Various people - as professionals or volunteers - come into prisons from the outside world. Mrs Sylvia Jefferson certainly had professional skills. She was a talented musician. For more than thirty years she played the organ in Crumlin Road Prison. But her contribution was much more than musical. With an approachable, friendly disposition she had the ability to relate to the prisoners. However if any tried to be a smart alec she could, with a few gracious but pointed words, make them crawl back into their shells. I often thought that such dedicated service deserved mention in the Honours' List.

Apart from Sunday services other activities took place. David Jardine and I held classes. In groups of between ten and fifteen, men met to discuss and grapple with questions of a religious nature. One day a prisoner asked me this question, 'How long have you to be saved before you die to get into heaven?' 'Five minutes, mate,' was my reply, 'but brother, do you know when you are going to die?'

Years later this prisoner told me that my answer really shook him. In the Maze he made a profession of faith but, I think, he lapsed. Addressing this prisoner by his name, one of his comrades, said straight out, 'You want the best of both worlds, but it doesn't work like that. You cannot live in a state of sin and of salvation at the same time.' Prisoners often read each other with shrewd insight.

In these discussions I gleaned examples of both spiritual ignorance and spiritual insight. Some surprised me by their knowledge of God's way of salvation.

At the Young Offenders' Centre the governor and his staff were most helpful in enabling me to bring guests along to the services, for I always tried to add interest by having a soloist or group along. Just as in Crumlin Road, the atmosphere was reverent. Few, if any, made a profession of faith. Nor did efforts by myself and others to start discussion classes meet with success. Yet in after years when I met any of them they remembered the services. Maybe their reasons were social rather than spiritual for, as I have said, they were able to converse before and after the services. In the context of the numbers of prisoners the visible signs of the fruits of the spirit may have been few, but in the context of eternity the one lost sheep who answers the Good Shepherd's call is of inestimable value.

I aimed to see the prisoners for whom I was responsible within their first 24 hours in jail. Afterwards I saw them in the workshop, gymnasium and wherever they happened to be. For their part, prisoners sometimes took the initiative and requested to see the chaplain, especially if there was a problem relating to home. 'You know, in here, molehills become mountains,' was how one summed it up.

I remember one prisoner whose wife stopped visiting him. He asked me to call at his home to find out why she had failed to come. When I managed to speak to her she promised she would be there next visiting day. She did not keep her promise. I called at the home again. No answer. Another week passed - and no visit. I called at the home another time. Although the door remained closed I had that intuitive feeling - often experienced by knockers of doors - that someone was inside, but had decided not to answer.

When I went back to Crumlin Road I said to the prisoner, 'Brother, I think the writing is on the wall .... she won't be visiting you again.' On meeting this man years later he turned to his mates and said, 'There is the man that told me the truth.'

Crumlin Road Prison - B Wing exercise yard

CHAPTER 13

VERSE AND PROSE

Nobody is likely to be shocked to learn that incarceration is followed by the details of the prisoner being documented in prose of the most pedestrian kind. Still, even prison cannot quench the human spirit. One of the greatest allegories in the English language - Bunyan's Pilgrim's Progress - was written in prison. Many of those imprisoned during Northern Ireland's troubles have shown remarkable creative talent as musicians, artists and writers. The prisoner who wrote the following poem would lay no claim to being a Bunyan, nor indeed a poetic genius of any kind. Nevertheless the poem gives a vivid insight into the horrendous shock that hits a man as he enters prison for the first time.

First Impressions

The banging of the prison gates,
As they leave my other life behind

Send thoughts of all my loved ones
Darting aimlessly through my mind.

The constant jingling of the warders' keys
Pull me sharply from my thought;
I regret all my actions,
But regret more being caught.

As I enter the reception,
I am met with angry leers
From the men who'll be my gaolers
For the next couple of years.

They start by documenting
All possessions and your health,
For here none of the men are poor
And none of them have wealth.

You begin to feel despondent
As you stare at all the walls,
And never see a friendly face
Until the prison chaplain calls.

He asks you what you're in for,
About your family kirk;
He writes down all the details of
Your life and where you work.

He takes a genuine interest
About the position that you're in,
And bows his head to say a prayer
For forgiveness for your sin.

He uses all his kindness
To relieve the burden on your head,
And replaces it with something else,
Something spiritual instead.

You don't need to be religious
To feel the power of the Saviour's hand,
And to feel the goodness emanating
From this ordinary man.

He lends a sympathetic ear,
And teaches you to share
The pangs of guilt and conscience
We sinners have to bear.

And finally he gives you hope
By the knowledge of God's Word,
That it is not a judge who gives you life,
But Jesus Christ, Our Lord.

I believe that this simple poem conveys something of the trauma that most prisoners experience upon imprisonment. Two lines strike me as especially poignant:

I regret now all my actions,
But I regret more being caught.

Here the poet very honestly admits that what makes him really sorry is being caught. There is no reference to the victims to whom he caused suffering. Nor is there any recognition of having broken the Divine Law and sinned against God.

For chaplains it is not always easy to distinguish between

Interior of a Prison Cell
(Hardly 4 Star!)

remorse and repentance. The prison authorities are pleased to see remorse. The chaplain has a different perspective. If a prisoner's 'remorse' goes no further than feeling sorry for his predicament, the chaplain understands the human feeling, but wants to see more. True repentance - a definite turning away from sin - and a realisation that sin is against God are what he looks for. The psalmist puts it this way: '*Against you, you only have I sinned and done what is evil in your sight.*' (Psalm 51:4 NIV).

The poet's reference to entering reception and meeting angry leers is a description of the officers who had to see that the men are examined and documented. The prisoners' personal details were carefully logged. Tattoos and birth-marks were noted and fingerprints taken. This unpleasant experience was concluded by allocating a number to the prisoner - a hard blow to personal dignity. (Some procedures, for example in relation to fingerprinting, have changed since I left the prison service.)

In Crumlin Road and older prisons where there were no toilet facilities in the cells, a slopping out parade took place each morning. Men tramped in a line of about twenty or thirty with their sanitary pots to the ablutions - a humbling and undignifying experience. I always tried to keep away from the wings during this exercise.

New prisoners varied in their attitude to life behind bars. Some set out to kick against the system. To such prisoners I tried to point out - kindly and gently - that in the end they would be the ones to suffer. The officers had a job to do; most did it in as sensitive and caring a way as was possible. Occasional clashes of personality were, I suppose, unavoid-able. In such cases both parties suffered.

When a prisoner did violate the prison regulations, he was reported to the principal officer on that wing. The governor heard and evaluated evidence presented by his staff. If the prisoner was found guilty of a misdemeanour, the governor could impose a range of sanctions. Permission to go to the tuck shop might be discontinued or confinement to the cell for a few days might be ordered. For a more serious offence a prisoner could be 'put on the boards.'

To be 'put on the boards' was to be put in a punishment cell similar in size to other cells, that is 9' x 7'. Built into one of the walls was a plank measuring 15" x 4". For the occupant this was table and chair. On another raised area was a mattress. Each evening this was brought in and each morning removed.

The Young Offenders' Centre had a raised platform 6' x 3' x 21/2', the last figure being the height. Secured to the wall was a seat like a toilet seat. So the prisoner had no chance of using the furniture as a weapon of destruction. In the cell the only movable object was a Bible. One prisoner told me that during his day in the cell he succeeded in reading I and II Samuel and Proverbs. Another prisoner told me he walked up and down the cell 5,000 times, took a rest, then repeated his walk, and so on until his day was over.

The other way of coping with imprisonment was to work according to the rules. This offered opportunities for making a positive contribution to prison life: preparing meals, keeping the wings and landings clean, gardening and suchlike jobs. At the Young Offenders Centre there were opportunities to paint, decorate, do woodwork and learn a trade.

At all the institutions men had access to education up to degree standard. Several left prison as graduates. Computers were installed creating yet further openings for leisure and education. There it was then: verse and prose and much else besides, all means of coping with incarceration and providing hope for a life beyond prison.

Chapter 14

Justice and Injustice

'Are innocent men ever sentenced to terms of imprisonment?' This is a question that I have often been asked. In Northern Ireland some people find the very concept of British justice absurd. While my background and upbringing have inclined me to have trust and confidence in British justice (and that still lingers with me), I fear that experience has led me to conclude that there can be miscarriages of justice. High profile political cases like the Birmingham Six and non-political cases like Timothy Evans give reason for reservation. But compared with the countless court proceedings I think that the instances of genuine miscarriages are extremely rare. No human system - political, ecclesiastical, educational, economic or judicial - is infallible. Perfect justice has to await '*the day when God will judge men's secrets through Jesus Christ*

(Romans 2:16).

Of course the idea of God's final exemplary judgment does not preclude the pursuit of legal redress here on earth, for the rights of the weak, poor, oppressed, fatherless and widowed is a persistent Biblical theme. One miscarriage of justice is one too many.

One controversial case with which I am acquainted is that of the ***UDR FOUR***. Winston Allen, Noel Bell, Jim Hegan and Neil Latimer were accused of the murder of Adrian Carroll in 1983. For their alleged part in this crime they were given life sentences. When they were remanded in custody in Crumlin Road Prison I was the chaplain. Over their $2^{1/2}$ years in custody I was in touch with all four conversing and discussing with them their stories. To me the case had many ramifications and innuendoes which raised doubts in my mind.

During his time on remand Jim Hegan worked consistently to prove his own and his colleagues' innocence. He was a Presbyterian, so I was his personal chaplain. Jim shared with me in great detail the background to his predicament and the wider implications of the whole episode. As I listened and analysed I became convinced that many circumstances surrounding their arrest and interrogation were a cause for concern and raised many uncomfortable questions. Even after many years I have not received satisfactory explanations and I remain uneasy in my mind.

While these men were on remand I was in touch with all their families who worked extremely hard to prove that their sons were innocent. In this they were helped by various people including the well-known author, broadcaster and journalist Robert Kee. Over the years the press gave a lot of publicity to the case and many articles - even books - have been written about the ***UDR FOUR***. Frequently - as opportunity occurred - I presented a list of the reasons why I considered that these men were not guilty. As for the parents, they said that if their boys had been guilty they would of course have stood by them, but would have accepted the justice of the court's sentence.

As is well-known three of the UDR FOUR were released on appeal. However as I write, Neil Latimer, now also released, has his appeal coming up soon.

So heavily did these matters weigh on my conscience even after my retirement from the prison chaplaincy that I took up my pen and wrote the following letter to Sir Patrick Mayhew, Secretary of State at the Northern Ireland Office.

14th February 1994
Sir Patrick Mayhew QC MP
Stormont Castle
BELFAST

Dear Sir Patrick

In 1982 I was installed by the above Church [the Presbyterian Church in Ireland] *as a full-time chaplain in the prisons: Crumlin Road, Hydebank Y.O.C., Maze and Maghaberry. While stationed in Crumlin Road the UDR men from Armagh were remanded in custody in December 1983 for the alleged murder of Adrian Carroll. Hence I am well acquainted with this case and its ramifications over the last ten years.*

I understand through the Press that an approach has been made to you on behalf of Neil Latimer, the one UDR man who is still incarcerated, to have his case brought to the Court of Appeal. Over my years as a chaplain I have come face to face with many prisoners and I have listened to many stories and tales. While seeking to take a genuine interest in these men I have always made it clear that wrong must be punished.

With that background, rightly or wrongly, I feel that there was a miscarriage of justice in the case of the UDR 4 and that the judgment was unsafe and unsound. If asked, there would be many reasons which I could give for coming to this conclusion.

I write this letter knowing that you will examine this case thoroughly; however I would appeal to you to scrutinize very carefully the evidence of Witness A which played an important part in the judgment.

Although retired and with absolutely no vested interest in this case, nevertheless for conscience sake I feel I must speak out where I fear there is an area of injustice.

Yours sincerely

J C BUICK

A few days later I received a simple acknowledgement of receipt of this letter from the Secretary of State's Private Office. It concluded with this promise: '*A reply will be forwarded to you as soon as possible.*' More than seven years later I am still awaiting the fulfilment of this promise.

It must be admitted that the task of the courts in deciding innocence or guilt is no easy one. Sometimes the verdict is clear-cut one way or the other and justice is seen to be done. But at other times something about the case in general or the verdict in particular sends ripples of disquiet through the community which may last for decades. The murder of Patricia Curran in 1952 is a case in point.

Another case with which I was familiar involved a man (whose name I now forget) who was accused of rape. His legal advice was that if he pleaded guilty his sentence would be less severe - probably seven years which, with remission, would have meant three and a half years. But this man's contention was that his partner was consenting, so naturally he went to court pleading not guilty. Imagine his dismay and shock when the court - obviously not believing him - imposed a sentence of 14 years.

When he was despatched to his cell I called to see him. After a short conversation about his sentence he asked me for a Bible. I gave him one. Next morning before he was transferred to the Maze I called to see him. Astonishingly he greeted me with the words, 'I am a Christian.' 'I am delighted to hear that,' I responded. I gave him some booklets on what it meant to be a Christian, prayed and wished him well.

Two years or so later I caught up with him again at Maghaberry Prison where he was still trying to lead a consistent Christian life though some of his professedly Christian mates were making life difficult for him. The last I heard of him he was continuing his journey with Christ. From time to time my mind goes back to him, for I cannot help but wonder how he is faring now.

CHAPLAIN WITH CRUMLIN ROAD PRISON STAFF

Chapter 15

Conmen and Conned men

To carry out my work in the prison service with some semblance of order I had to keep records. My only regret is that these records were not fuller and more meticulous than they were, for the different characters with whom I had contact were legion, numbering into four figures. When the number of contacts goes beyond the thousand, what a variety of human experience is represented there! Needless to say it is impossible to remember them all, but I do have memories of certain individuals with gifts and abilities that made me feel how tragic it was that even for a short period they found themselves deprived of their freedom. Had it not been for The Troubles, I contend, without fear of contradiction, that many of the men I interviewed would never have seen the inside of a prison.

Some of the younger men were manipulated by more sinister individuals who often managed to evade the law. These 'godfathers,' usually operating from the pubs and clubs, managed to inveigle recruits into the paramilitary organisations.

I remember one young married man who shared his story with me. He had gone into a pub to have a beer with his pals. Probably this was part of his life style. On this occasion his meeting with his loyalist mates, whose views he shared, was to have an unhappy outcome. He was now in contact with men who were involved in terrorist crime. Another action was being planned. Transport was needed. This young man - with his life ahead of him - was prevailed upon to drive the vehicle from A to B. Whether this was his own vehicle or not I do not know, nor do I know all the details of what happened. Whatever part he did play in what was a serious crime was sufficient to earn him a lengthy prison sentence. During his confinement he would frequently say how sorry he was that he called in the pub for a beer that day.

Another story came from an actual publican. He was embroiled in a robbery in which valuable antiques were stolen. His role was to provide a hiding place for the stolen property. As I listened to his long, complicated narrative I thought I was eavesdropping on a detective story from a unique angle. This man's crime resulted in him losing his business, home and wife. In addition he had to serve a protracted sentence.

In prison there were what were termed the ODCs - ordinary decent criminals, though I hardly think that victims considered them such. After all car theft, assault, 'joy' riding, and breaking and entering represent human suffering. So too does failure to pay maintenance in the case of broken marriages. However the 'decent' criminals normally accepted their punishment and tried to come to terms with their new life style. Their burning desire was to get their sentence over and back to the outside world. This longing to be released and back home was called Gate Fever.

Undeniably some men found themselves in a predicament through being conned by others; that meant of course that there had to be conmen. Sometimes prisoners were suspected of 'converting' to Christianity so that they might improve their chances of early release. No doubt this did happen. Whether they played the religious game or some other ruse to gain sympathy - and more likely than not money - these conmen tended to have certain characteristics in common. Upon meeting them they were all sweetness and light. They had a story which they could tell with charm, fluency and, if deemed appropriate, pathos. So persuasive were they that I sometimes wondered if they had succeeded in deceiving themselves. Rightly or wrongly I concluded that the more resplendent the story and more suave the narrator, the more likely he was to be a conman.

Of course as a minister I have met conmen (and a few conwomen too) outside as well as inside prison. Each 'hard luck' story needs a careful appraisal. While no Christian wants to turn away someone in genuine need, neither does one want to be taken for a fool, nor, worse still, assist someone into further folly. It depends on the circumstances and upon one's intuition.

Many years ago a man approached me with a sorrowful, tear-jerking tale about his mother being seriously ill and in need of him. He asked me for the bus fare to travel from Belfast to Cookstown where his mother lived. I listened to him very attentively.

Summing up the situation I said, 'That's a very convincing story but to be honest, I fear you are a conman. I tell you what I'll do. In my wallet I have paper money, either in £5 or

£10 notes. If I have a £5 note I'll give it to you but if I have only a £10 note I won't be giving you £10.' I opened my wallet and showed it to him. Only £10 notes were in it.

'Sorry. Goodbye,' were, I think, my parting words. Afterwards I still considered I had done the right thing, for in my estimation he was an out-and-out conman.

One of my contemporaries developed his own strategy for dealing with those who came begging money for a meal. Instead of responding directly he gave the supplicant his card on which he wrote a message. The idea was that the beggar could present the card to a restaurant owner who would ring my friend and be reimbursed for the cost of the meal. This method is not without its own flaws and indeed my colleague was not able to follow this practice on every occasion.

He tells of one encounter of how he was sitting in his car near shops when he was approached by a man who asked him for money. 'If I give you money you'll only spend it on booze.' This was a standard response of my friend to such requests. 'No,' the man replied. 'Do you see that butcher's shop over there? I'll go in there and buy sausages for a meal.'

My friend gave in. With the money in his hand the man went across to the butcher's. In he went, my friend watching from his car. As the man left the shop and came into sight he held up a paper bag, waved it towards my friend and disappeared from view. Curiosity got the better of the good Samaritan. Into the butcher's he proceeded. 'Excuse me,' he mumbled. 'Do you mind if I ask what that man who has just gone out bought?' 'Nothing,' replied the butcher. 'He only asked me for a paper bag.'

Chapter 16

Consolations and Rewards

My morning routine as a chaplain in Crumlin Road Prison started between 8.30 am and 9.00 am. Often I then proceeded to the basement to meet the new inmates who had been to court the previous day and had either been sentenced or remanded in custody. According to prison regulations, on the first morning after incarceration a prisoner was due to be seen by a governor, a doctor, a dentist, a social worker and a chaplain.

One morning as I was scanning my list of names I noted that of a particular prisoner. I shall call him Joe Jones though that was not his real name. A few weeks earlier I had interviewed a prisoner with an identical surname; let us give him the first name Bill.

This gave me a natural opening. 'Are you related to Bill

Jones?' I asked Joe.'Oh yes,' he replied, 'Bill is my brother.'

Our conversation continued for a time, roving over many topics. I kept thinking of the mother who had now two sons in prison. 'Have you nothing between your ears to get yourself in here?' I eventually expostulated. 'Wouldn't it be enough for your parents to cope with, to have one of you in here?'

Joe went on to tell me what happened. 'I was in a bar,' he said, 'when these men started mouthing about my brother and his alleged crime. I could stick it no longer. I lifted the chair I was sitting on and walloped all around me, and, as a result, here I am.'

I listened. How many times had I heard similar stories? 'Now that you are in here,' I proceeded, ''try to accept the fact of being in prison. Whatever you do, don't kick against the system because in the end you'll be the one that's the loser.'

He heard me out without saying much more. I left him in no doubt that I believed that wrong deserved to be punished.

During this period of confinement Joe behaved reasonably well, even coming to an occasional Sunday service. But when he got out of prison, it was only for a short time. For several years Joe used the revolving door at the prison. Drink was his weakness. One night at a band parade in Bushmills - so I was told - it took four policemen to get him into a Land-Rover.

In an interlude between spells in prison I visited Joe at his home, fifty miles from Belfast. There he was in the backyard sawing up a telegraph pole to make blocks. By selling these he hoped to make a few pounds.

As I chatted with him that day I suggested that this way of life was lacking purpose and meaning. There are plenty of men like you,' I ventured, quoting the old maxim, 'When the wine's in, the wit's out.'

I told him about Ted Frampton whose victory over

worldliness including gambling is recounted elsewhere in this book. 'The God who regenerated Ted Frampton could do the same for you,' I declared.

Here was a sturdy young man who had no fear, who could handle himself in a fight yet who underneath a rough, tough exterior had a quality that won my affection. Whether I prayed with him or not, I do not remember but I did tell him that Christ loved him and died to save him. I reiterated my basic message of Christ's abundant and abounding mercy. 'In Christ,' I said, 'there are all the resources to make you a new creature.' So I took my leave.

The next place I met Joe was in Wandsworth Prison in London! In May 1990 the Northern Ireland Office had arranged for me to visit eight institutions on the mainland. Wandsworth was one of these. Bill told me that his brother Joe was there. When Joe was brought into the chaplain's office to meet me, he threw his arms around me. What followed was among those prison visits that I could log as worthwhile and positive.

A decade passed before our paths crossed again. In December 2000 I came upon Joe with residents of The Haven moving a cooker from Glengormley to their place at Rickamore near Loanends Presbyterian Church.

The Haven may need a word of explanation. It is a Christian Centre based on an idea found in 1st Samuel 22. David had fled to the cave of Adullam to escape the wrath of King Saul. Verse two of the chapter reads: '*All those who were in distress or in debt or discontented gathered around him and he became their leader ...*' In broad terms The Haven reaches out to those who had fallen on hard times.

Like others, Joe Jones came to The Haven through some-one who cared enough. In a supportive environment he is maturing into responsible Christian manhood. Joe is the first to acknowledge his indebtedness to Hunter Kirk and the staff at the Haven.

When I got talking to Joe on that December day the first thing he told me was that three years previously God had saved him. Here was a man who had a record of sixty-six charges of assault against policemen now speaking of salvation and, what's more, his own salvation. He had served time in all five men's prisons in Northern Ireland as well as in two in Scotland and three in England, including Wandsworth where I had met him. After this wild, wayward life God had caught up with him in dynamic fashion.

Despite his obstinacy and frequent relapses Joe maintains that God was working in his life through it all. He may have been trying to escape God, but God was chasing - and closing in on - him.

From the different incidents in his life Joe recalls being involved in an ACE scheme with Jackie McKee on the Shankill Road. For Joe the Haven - a place of refuge from the storm - was indeed well named.

Upon arrival at The Haven Joe admits that he felt insecure. Life was unhappy ... without a purpose. He hated himself for the antics and escapades into which he had allowed himself to be drawn. He had come to a critical point. God was unmistakeably working in his life. For Joe the encounter with the Eternal was not through a bright light from heaven, nor yet through '*a still small voice.*' Joe's own words were, 'God broke me.'

For Joe, to be a Christian in the Biblical sense was demanding. Letters of apology had to be written - the first of which was to his mother - and debts - amounting to about £2,000 - had to be paid. Joe did not shirk the responsibility. Physically, mentally, emotionally and spiritually he set about the task, not only clearing the debt but managing to become the owner of fifteen cows and hold down a steady job.

In the Church Fellowship to which he belongs Joe takes an active part. Earlier this year (2001) he was on an outreach team to Portugal and from what I hear was the life and soul of the party - enthusiastic and constructive in his contribution. Of course becoming a Christian did not mean the disappearance of his troubles.

'Life has been far from being a bed of roses,' confesses Joe. The important point is that he is trusting the Lord to guide and keep him through the good times and the bad.

Over my ten years in prisons many men attended the services and classes arranged by the chaplains. Earlier I implied that conversions were few, that is, as a proportion of the prison population. However, of those who did profess faith in Christ, most - I believe - were sincere.

As in the world at large the Parable of the Sower is an apt analysis of the ground on which prison chaplains were sowing seed. The seed which fell by the wayside was quickly picked up by the birds of indifference, ignorance and unresponsiveness, hence it was unfruitful. The seed which fell on the stoney places of bitterness, hatred and dogmatism fared little better. When the sun shone, the shallowness of any momentary signs of spiritual life withered while temptations flourished. The seed which fell among the thorns of selfishness, avarice and deceitfulness was soon choked, again making insignificant growth.

Yet some seed did fall on good ground. The chaplain's earnest prayer is that this seed will go on to produce *'a crop - a hundred, sixty or thirty times what was sown.'*

In a book of this size it is impossible to include accounts of all the incidents and individuals that I have encountered. It would however be remiss of me not to acknowledge my appreciation of the help, encouragement, counsel and guidance I received from the governors under whom I have served.

I go further. I enjoyed all my contacts with all the staff of all the institutions in which I worked. Had circumstances permitted I would have been delighted to have given more years to the prison service. I felt I was in the place of God's purpose. I trusted that I was being used as an instrument of his blessing to those to whom I ministered. Despite frustrations and disappointments work has always had its consolations and rewards.

Another place of consolation and reward was - and remains - home and family. It is all too easy to take domestic blessings for granted. What a blessing it is to know that my wife has been at one with me all along the life's journey! Daisy recalls a little - a very little - of her personal pilgrimage in Chapter Nineteen, so here, in a few paragraphs, I come back to our son, Raymond.

One of Solomon's proverbs goes, *'A wise son maketh a glad father.'* As Raymond grew up - in an age with fewer temptations than now - he never caused his mother or myself needless worry.

As I mentioned earlier, he attended Everton Primary School, then the Boys' Model. One night at bedtime he told his mother that he wanted to be a doctor. Though he was only about ten years old, he obviously meant it, for he went on to Queen's University, Belfast from which, in 1972, he graduated in Medicine. Then, in1976, he qualified as a Fellow of the College of Surgeons.

In 1978 Raymond married Dr Jennifer Williamson in Garvagh Presbyterian Church where her father, the Rev John Williamson, was the minister.

For the past sixteen years Raymond and Jennifer have been living in Birmingham. Raymond is one of the consultant paediatric surgeons in Birmingham Children's Hospital. Jennifer is an associate specialist in women's health in the City Hospital, Birmingham.

They have three boys. Michael graduated from Oxford University in June 2001 but is continuing his studies in Art and History aiming for further qualifications. Jonathan has been accepted by the University of Bristol to study Environmental Geoscience. Alastair is in his final year at Cadbury College working for his A-levels.

The whole family is involved in St John Parish Church, Harbourne. They feel very much at home in the life and work of the church there.

DR. RAYMOND & MRS JENNIFER BUICK

The Grandchildren:
Michael, Jonathan and Alastair

Chapter 17

Outreaches and Inroads

From the records that I have kept during my ministry I see that I have conducted sixty-five missions or other evangelistic outreaches. Forty-five of these lasted two weeks, the other twenty between four and ten days. Fifty-eight were conducted in Presbyterian churches, the rest in an assortment of buildings. Most took place within the province of Ulster: from Castlewellan to Coleraine, from Larne to Letterkenny. A few entailed journeys outside the province.

If possible, I liked to return home each night. Usually this was possible though it could mean a lot of driving. For one two-week mission the car recorded 1,500 miles, most of it with me behind the wheel.

The invitation to take part in some special outreach normally came from fifteen to eighteen months before the cam paign. This gave time for planning and preparation.

I always asked for my first contact with the congregation to be with the Kirk Session for, after all, their responsibility is the spiritual oversight of the congregation. Next I tried to meet the midweek gathering or prayer group. With the help of the elders I liked to do a whistle-stop tour of the congregation before the mission actually started. During this visitation I called with the housebound and conducted a simple Act of Worship. In this way I was able to gauge the spiritual temperature of the congregation. I believe these visits also added to the warmth of the services.

Final preparations took place in my study. There I sought God's guidance and worked on my sermons. I prayed that I might be enabled to present the Gospel with grace and graciousness.

Inside my head I distinguished three groups of people. From God's viewpoint there were of course only two groups - believers and unbelievers. But from the human standpoint I could see a third group - those who were uncertain of their standing before Christ.

For the believers - whose presence and support were appreciated - my prayer was that they would be encouraged, even excited, to witness and share their faith. For the unbeliever the priority was obvious: salvation.

It is the third group that often intrigues me most. Often these people are faithful in attendance on at least one Sunday service, and supportive of church functions. Some are even involved in the work of committee, or help in an organisation or Sunday school. On many matters they may be quite talkative but when it comes to issues of faith they are remarkably reticent. If they are challenged outright as to whether or not they are Christians, they usually answer, 'I hope I am' or words to that effect. To go beyond that and say, for instance, 'I am saved,' or 'I am a born-again believer' is in their estimation being presumptuous and dogmatic. Presbyterians are not renowned for wearing their faith on their sleeve.

What is the explanation for this phenomena? Maybe they have been confronted in an unnecessarily aggressive manner by someone proclaiming in an accusing way 'You must be born again' or questioned as if at a tribunal, 'Are you saved?' To compound the offence, the would-be winner of souls may exhibit in his home or business life the works of the flesh rather than the fruit of the spirit. Jesus said, *'Ye shall know them by their fruits. Do men gather grapes of thorns or figs of thistles'* (Matt 7:16).

Another reason for lack of assurance may be lack of faith in the first place. A third possibility is that the doctrine of assurance is no longer preached. In his book ***Learning and Living the Christian Life,*** G R Harding-Wood puts it bluntly, *'In hundreds of pulpits today the doctrine of assurance is either not preached or even is denied. All this is sadly true in spite of the Word of Gods which says, "These things have I written unto you that ye may* ***know*** *that ye have eternal life."'* It is a sobering thought that since 1953 when the book was first published, the sermon has continued to be under attack. In the missions I conducted I could but preach the Word trusting that it would accomplish that which God pleased including giving assurance to those who lacked it.

To be responsible for outreach and evangelism did not rest lightly on my shoulders. I tried to combine faithfulness to God and to His Word with sensitivity and love towards the congregations to whom I ministered.

Before I accepted an invitation to conduct a mission I made it clear that I was limited in the technique - or whatever term you apply to it - of issuing an appeal for anxious souls to come forward at the close of the service. 'While every head is bowed .... ' may be for other evangelists. Billy Graham and Luis Palau have not eschewed the invitation system and I had no theological or other objections to making an appeal for an outward response at the conclusion of a service. But the truth is that on those rare occasions when I did call for a visible demonstration the response was limited.

Indeed there were missions for which there had been careful practical preparation and earnest seeking of God in prayer. During the services there existed a reverent, listening attitude. Yet so often there was little evidence of spiritual awakening. Why this should be, perplexed me.

Even allowing for the fact that Presbyterian missions are often attended by the faithful, I could hardly imagine that every single person on every single night was already saved. To be frank I was disappointed. Self-examination left me with the lurking fear that I had failed in preparation. Or maybe I was not the person suited to making spiritual inroads into the life of this congregation or that community.

However, it was not all doom and gloom. Here and there the light of the gospel flickered or even shone brightly. One minister judged that the mission in his church had resulted in the ethos of his congregation being radically changed with a new priority on evangelism.

Now that I am in retirement I meet people who say they had been helped to find Christ at a particular meeting. Recently I met a lady who, twenty-five years previously, had attended a mission in which I had been the evangelist. She told me that she and her husband - then young people - had both been converted at that mission. It was the first I knew of it.

How God has used any of us to be an influence for Christ will be known only hereafter. I count it a privilege to have been involved in outreach and humbled that God has used me even in a small way to make inroads into sinful lives.

Chapter 18

Sharing and Caring

As I come near the end of these reminiscences I want to return to some of the organisations and institutions with which I have been and still am associated. Mostly these are made up of people whose aim is to share the gospel or care for those to whom life has dealt a blow. In recent years I have had the privilege of seeing some of these organisations and institutions from a different perspective.

The Belfast City Mission

In 1988 the Executive Secretary of the Belfast City Mission, William Cooke, informed me that I had been appointed to the Governing Body of the Mission. Shortly afterwards I was appointed Superintendent of the new work in the Ballyduff estate and joined the other members on the Superintendents' Board. I was delighted to be returning in an active capacity to a work in which I had been a missionary in the prime years of my life. By one of those singularities of providence, which I had experienced before, I was recently invited to be superintendent of Bilston Road Hall - an honour indeed for it brought me back to the Ballysillan area where I had started.

Another responsibility came my way about three years ago. The Very Rev Dr John Girvan retired as Honorary Secretary and, as Elijah's mantle was taken up by Elisha, so John Girvan's was taken up by me. In this position I am kept in contact with the work of the Mission as a whole. One of my tasks is to go through the twenty-one reports of the missionaries and compile an annual report. This gives me an insight into the labours of these men.

The format of the Belfast City Mission is as it has been over the years. Priority is still given to personal evangelism with the missionaries tramping the streets as I did half-a-century ago. Thousands of tracts and booklets are distributed. And there are still the weekly meetings in the halls.

In 1998 a missionary was appointed to the city centre. Though this man does not hold meetings at stated times, he has the use of a small hall in Berry Street Presbyterian Church. He regularly visits St George's Market and keeps in contact with taxi drivers. He also maintains contact with those who, because of their pattern of life, live rough or are homeless.

Times have changed since those days of my outreach work in Belfast. Life on the street is more hazardous, drugs are prevalent, and of course The Troubles have left their distressing legacy. Altogether there is greater hostility to Christianity. Nevertheless God remains sovereign, and missionaries are still privileged to see His grace at work as those with no hope are transformed, proving that if any man is in Christ he is a new creature. The greater the godlessness of society, the greater is the need for evangelism.

It comes as a surprise to many people to learn that the Belfast City Mission is financed largely by voluntary gifts from individuals, churches and organisations.

The mission has an office in Church House, Fisherwick Place, Belfast BT1 6DW. The website is www.belfastcitymission.com

CHRISTIAN ENDEAVOUR

The seventh question to Presbyterian ministers who are being ordained or installed is: *Having accepted the call of this congregation, do you promise through Divine grace to make full proof of your ministry among them, preaching the Gospel of the grace of God, administering the sacraments, visiting the people, catechising and instructing the young, visiting the sick, aiding in the government of the Church, and discharging all other duties incumbent upon you as a Minister of Jesus Christ.*

Those who sincerely seek to keep such a promise soon discover that the ministry is truly a full-time job. The variety of commitments is a sure guarantee against boredom. Yet I, like most of my colleagues, find that contacts with the world beyond the congregation can be refreshing. They also act as an antidote against parochialism and introversion. However the extent of these responsibilities needs to be meticulously monitored and controlled.

Earlier I acknowledged my indebtedness as a youth to the Christian Endeavour. I joined First Antrim CE as an associate member in the mid-1930s. When I became a Christian that was where I was nursed, nurtured and helped to mature.

In later years I have maintained a connection with this movement. I did a spell as national lookout convener. For twenty years or more I have been the national Seniors' and

Comrades' convener and a member of the National Council. I am also privileged to have served a term as president.

The story of Christian Endeavour started like many good stories - and, it must be admitted, some bad ones - in the United States. In January 1881 the Rev Francis E Clark held a series of services in his Williston Congregational Church, Portland, Maine. At these meetings many - one estimate puts it at fifty - young people were converted. For the mutual support of these newly converted Christians Francis Clark had the idea - which, he claimed, came to him directly from heaven - of a Young Peoples' Society of Christian Endeavour. In the words of the CE historian, Dudley L Cooney, *'it was not a group of young people endeavouring to be Christians, but a group of young Christians endeavouring, that is doing their best in Christian service.'* A nice but crucial distinction.

In the 120 years since its birth Christian Endeavour has expanded into a worldwide organisation. Though its structures and activities have been modified with the times, the underlying ethos remains close to that of its originator.

The first CE Society in Ireland got off the ground in Agnes Street Presbyterian Church in 1889. The founder was Miss Margaret Magill. Ten years later CE membership in Ireland reached ten thousand. Between 1920 and 1940 the Movement was at its zenith. In Castle Erin holiday home in Portrush the photographs of conventions in the early 1930's testify to its strength in those days. Today CE still provides a training for young people who become ministers, missionaries and youth workers.

In an excellent recently published information leaflet CE is described as Christ-centred and Church-based. Further adjectives designate it as all-age, action-packed, challenging, international and interdenominational. Then using verbs the leaflet indicates that CE helps young people reach, hold, teach, train and equip. It is nearly as big a commitment as that demanded by that seventh question I have answered on several occasions during my ministry.

The Northern Ireland headquarters of Christian Endeavour is Bank House, 135 Albertbridge Road, Belfast BT5 4RS. The website is www.ceireland.org

SOCIAL WITNESS

For many years I have had a close association with the work of the Social Witness Board of our church. This has included membership of its Alcohol and Drug Education Committee which aims to combat the growing tide of alcohol and drug abuse in society and oppose the relaxing of social legislation in ways that enable the drinks' industry to target younger people

I am still a member and Chairman of the Thompson House Management Committee which is responsible for a hostel for ex-prisoners and the administration of the Boys' Residential Club fund. This fund started as a bequest in the name of the Rev W J Thompson.

In the last ten years the Social Witness Board has come more to the fore in the life of the Presbyterian Church in Ireland. Those who formulated paragraph 281 of the Code had great vision and a sense of compassion when they stipulated that the Board *"concern itself with all questions affecting the social welfare of the Church and the community."*

Today, with about 380 employees the Board of Social Witness is responsible for an annual budget of £4,000,000. Its diverse work embraces the care of older people through the Presbyterian Residential Trust, the Kinghan Mission for deaf people, a wide range of alcohol and drug related activities and measures aimed at helping long term unemployed people to find jobs. The Board also administers the War Memorial Hostel Fund through which it now operates a mission to students in the Queen's University area of Belfast. This is based at Derryvolgie Hall, a complex of flats for 88 students, where a vibrant Christian community is led by the Rev Steve Stockman.

In 2001 the Board opened its first supported housing scheme for people with learning disabilities in Coleraine. This aims to provide a sympathetic Christian environment for people who are either no longer able to live with their own families, or simply want to have their own homes in the community. The Rev Jim Waring, formerly Minister of Ballyrashane congregation, heads this new work.

Since 2000 the Board of Social Witness has been responsible for the Marriage and the Family Committee. In a confidential setting counselling is available to couples who are having relationship problems. With marriage breakdowns on the increase even within our church family, this service is needed more than ever. Where one of a couple planning marriage has been previously married, the Panel on Remarriage interviews the two of them before the knot is tied. With divorces also more numerous in our church, it is important that a second (or third) marriage is not entered into lightly. Ministers often wrestle with this problem, but many welcome the service provided by the Panel on Remarriage.

The Social Witness Board publishes resources to help church members to gain a Biblical perspective on some of the complicated social issues that today receive so much cover in the media. In the not too distant past certain social and sexual issues were mentioned only seldom and even then in whispers; that is no longer the case. Homosexuality, euthanasia, abortion, the perplexing condition of eating disorders and the effect that childlessness can have on a young couple are some of the issues on which our Social Issues and Resources Committee has produced recent guidance.

The Social Witness Board is sometimes thought of merely as the caring side of the church's work, majoring on the provision of social care. The Board, however, does not see things in that light. The Board is deeply committed to the wider vision of the Presbyterian Church, believing that social witness and evangelism are both vital and inseparably aspects of mission. This may not have been well enough taught and understood over the years, resulting in some of our members thinking of social witness as only for those who were less than comfortable with more direct forms of evangelism. Personally, my years in prison chaplaincy and with the Board of Social Witness leave me in no doubt that most people do not pay much attention to what we know, until they realize that we genuinely care about them and the human needs that they are experiencing.

THOMPSON HOUSE

Thompson House is an interesting example of a group of Christians identifying a human need to which a Board of the Church responds in a practical way. In this case, I and other prison chaplains were concerned about the number of men who left prison in the 1970s with nowhere to live. The results were obvious. The men re-offended and ended up back in prison. The need was not for more evangelists and better preaching, it was for beds and an environment in which the dignity of men leaving prison would be respected. Yes, we believed then, and still do, that ex-prisoners are God's creatures and that they should experience His love just as much as unconverted Presbyterians!

In 1983 money that had been set aside following the closure of the Boys' Residential Club in Finaghy in the late 1960s was used to purchase a property on the Antrim Road, Belfast so that a hostel for male ex-prisoners could be opened. Needless to say, it was not that simple. The Board of Social Witness had no experience of this kind of development and we had not nearly enough money to see the project through. A committee was formed. The knowledge and contacts that Sammy Chapman and others had in the Northern Ireland Office and the Probation Service were used to obtain advice and financial support. Thompson House was opened on 28th April 1994 by the then Moderator of the General Assembly the Right Reverend T J Simpson.

In 1992 an adjacent property was purchased and renovated to provided six flats for men who have lived for a period in the hostel and are ready to live more independently, before getting their own home in the community. This was named the McCormick Suite after the late Sydney McCormick who, until his premature death, had been Director of Thompson House.

Thompson House is different in many ways from much of the work that goes on in our church. Most of those who come there have experienced alienation throughout their lives and they have little or no understanding of Christian values. They come from backgrounds characterised by mistrust. The idea that anyone would trust, let alone love, them is foreign to their thinking. The concept of God's love is just beyond the comprehension of many of the residents.

It is the task of our staff, led by David Farrow, an elder in the Glengormley Church, to care for the men in a practical way and to demonstrate dignity, trust and understanding. We say that people do not care what we know, until they know that we care. That is what Thompson House is all about. The men who come to live there are rejected by society.

Paramilitary support organisations do not want to know them and most communities do not want them either. The question we ask ourselves is, *"What would Christ have done, had he been faced with the same situation as prison chaplains are?"* I believe that Thompson House is an expression of the Gospel and one that our church can be proud of, in the right sense, of course.

The web site for the Board of Social Witness is:- www.presbyterianireland.org/bsw

CHAPTER 19

ABUNDANT AND ABOUNDING

The title of my life story is Abundant and Abounding. I use this title again for this penultimate chapter, for what has struck me most during my eighty years has been the amazing nature of God's grace not only in my own life but in the lives of others. Here are further accounts of that abundant and abounding mercy at work in the lives of a few of the people I have met in various places. Some have already had brief mention in earlier chapters but others are appearing for the first time.

TED AND LILY FRAMPTON
RECOUNTED BY LILY

As a teenager I was invited to attend a local mission and heard the gospel preached. Afterwards I went into the enquiry room, not because of what I had heard but because my friend decided to go forward and I didn't want to appear different. The charade ended in a few days. Nothing had happened because I wasn't in earnest. I thought to myself, stifling my conscience, "I will become a Christian if I don't get a husband!" I wasn't aware then of the verse in the Bible which warns, *"Do not boast about tomorrow, for you do not know what a day may bring forth"* (Proverbs 27:1).

As it turned out, I did get a husband. A little boy was born some time later and life was kind. After a while when the war was over, my husband Ted was demobbed from The Royal Ulster Rifles and came home to work in the shipyard. He had been steeped in the things of the world for many years in the army, and after a period he was soon involved in gambling. I could see that our marriage was in danger. At that time my close friend Annie Frampton, my husband's sister, accepted Christ as her Saviour in the 1945 mission, held in Ligoniel City Mission Hall, and invited us to attend the meeting. I went with her but Ted couldn't be persuaded. For several weeks I enjoyed the friendliness of the people and the rousing singing. However I became very uncomfortable, when the evangelist Jackson Buick invited folk to trust the Lord Jesus. I'm ashamed to say that I took the coward's way out and stopped going. That was not the answer. There followed a period of such misery that Ted said I was becoming hard to live with and "I had better get back to that hall to see what they could do for me."

At Easter in 1947 I went back and could hardly wait for Jackson to issue the invitation. I remember him saying, "Who do you want to deal with you?" My reply was, that I didn't mind who spoke to me, so long as I got peace. This was my second time to enter an enquiry room – the first as a teenager with no conviction of sin, and now as a married woman with a great burden and a sincere desire to get right with God. A gentleman named Jim Pedlow opened the scriptures to me and I received the peace I craved. He showed me that God could give me '*peace which passes all understanding.*' When I accepted Christ as my Saviour that night, I received His *peace*, *pardon* and *power*, and the assurance that He would never leave me. The only problem on the horizon was how to break the news to Ted. I felt that I should tell him the truth. He reacted by simply saying, "Don't preach at me." I didn't, but along with all the other believers in the Hall I earnestly prayed that God would touch his life and convict him of his sin. Three months later I witnessed a miracle – Ted on his knees crying to God for His salvation. Space forbids the telling of the years which followed; suffice to say that the Lord directed us to become evangelists to the Forces with the work of The Soldiers' and Airmen's Scripture Readers Association (SASRA) and then gave us household salvation when our son Malcolm accepted Christ as his Saviour at the age of six.

Our first posting was for four years to Catterick Camp, Yorkshire, where the Lord blessed and taught us much. There followed a tour in Singapore, where again He saved many servicemen and women. Then the unexpected happened. Our son Malcolm tragically died at the age of sixteen. It was a devastating blow. Up until then I had always said, "The Lord is able to save." Now we could say, "The Lord is able to keep." Yes, He kept us as He promised.

Our next posting was back to England in 1962, followed by a number of four-year tours around the country, where God was pleased to bless His word to men and women in the Services. Then came December 1978 and our retirement from London, with no home to go to. The Lord's promise held firm *"And my God shall supply all your need according to His riches in glory by Christ Jesus"* (Philippians 4:19). Much prayer brought the answer in the form of a beautiful little thatched cottage in a Hampshire village. Having spent eight wonderful years there, without warning I suffered a cardiac arrest whilst a passenger in the car. Miraculously we were only a quarter of a mile from the hospital when it happened and Ted managed to get me there in time.

We resumed life at a slower pace and thanked God each day for His goodness. One of the highlights of our retirement was that we were able to renew fellowship with our friends in Northern Ireland in August of each year. We went back in 1996 with our usual anticipation of blessing. It was during that time that Ted was unexpectedly called Home. The shock was almost too much to bear and my immediate reaction was that I wanted to go too. God was in control, however, and while I did not know what to do, He did, because He knows the end from the beginning. The friends from Shankill Baptist Church arranged his funeral and others came from mission days and took part in the service. I can truly say that the

Lord was in every detail. I wondered then about the future, and life without Ted. Since that time I've had some low moments but it always comes to me that I cannot go any lower than *"the everlasting arms underneath me"* (Deut 33:27). None of us knows what the future holds, but praise God, I know the One who holds the future.

As I reflect, I have often thought back to those early days in Belfast and to the chain of events that occurred when Ted and I accepted Jesus as our Saviour. In God's pattern for our lives, I can see that people like Jackson Buick were strategically placed by the Lord and played a huge part in our spiritual growth. I trust that as we all look back in years to come, we will testify to having met faithful servants like Jackson, who do not seek glory for themselves but would rather simply be classed as signposts pointing to the Saviour.

JAMES AND ELIZABETH MCKEEMAN
RECOUNTED BY EACH IN TURN

First James's Testimony

I was brought up in a home where my parents took me to church regularly and I attended Sunday School and the Boys' Brigade. I tried to live what I thought was a good life.

When I left school my ambition was to make money and live an upright life. I was never mixed up with alcohol or smoking. For as long as I can remember there was never a time when I didn't believe there was a God.

Shortly after I married, the Rev Drew Moore came to minister in Toberkeigh Presbyterian Church and through the exposition of God's Word I now realized that the Holy Spirit was speaking to me - so much so that I began to attend the midweek meeting. At that time I had twin girls and was concerned how I would teach them in the things of God.

A mission was held in the church in 1979 conducted by the Rev Jackson Buick and by the first Wednesday I realized that I was not right with God and needed to be saved. Following a visit to our home by Mr Buick and Mr Jim Chestnutt, I stayed behind after the mission meeting that evening and yielded my life to Christ. I immediately experienced the peace of God in my heart.

At times things have not been easy on the farm but I can lean on God's promise, for, *"I know that in all things God works for the good of all who love Him, who have been called according to His purpose"* (Romans 8:28).

As I look back I realize that it is possible to be lost and not know it because I was heading for a lost eternity and was unaware of it.

My wife and I are so grateful to God for the encouragement we have received from Jim and the late Mrs June Chestnutt in our early Christian life. They brought us to meetings where we shared our testimony and this strengthened us spiritually.

And now Elizabeth's Testimony

I was brought up in the Church of Ireland and from an early age was sent to Sunday School and Church. I was involved in all the church activities but never involved in the more gross sins of the world. I got married and never doubted that all was well with my soul until a mission came to our area run by the Faith Mission Pilgrims. At one of these meetings a very close friend challenged me concerning my spiritual need. I rebelled taking the attitude that I lived my life as best I could and couldn't see what difference being saved would make.

I believe at that time God had started to deal with me because my husband and I both thought that we should go to the prayer meeting in our church, and so we did.

In February 1979 the Rev Jackson Buick started a mission in the church and on the fourth evening in his message said, 'You are either a saint or a sinner, either saved or lost and you cannot sit on the fence. There is no middle ground.'

At the end of the meeting we both waited behind. Mr Buick prayed with us and led us to the Lord. Hallelujah!

Since then I have sought to serve Him realizing that unless He gives me power I can do nothing. I have failed Him many times but He has never failed me. I thank the Lord that long before I knew Him, He had thought of me. His grace is sufficient to meet all my needs and I have proved it many times since I was saved.

JAMES COCHRANE
RECOUNTED BY HIMSELF

I was brought up in a church going family. From an early age I went to Sunday school and church. This was a way of life for me.

Being brought up on a farm meant hard work and not much time to think about education. It was home from school and straight out to help on the farm.

At fifteen years of age I left school and went to serve my time in a shoe shop. This turned out to be my career and I am still selling shoes today.

In time I married and now have two of a family, a daughter and a son. We enjoyed family life and this involved going to church on Sunday as usual. I joined the church bowling club and later was elected to serve on the church committee. In 1978 our minister, the Rev T H Mullin, retired. We called one of these evangelical ministers, the Rev Graham Connor. I was not terribly interested in what he had to say, found fault with the length of his sermons etc and was generally opposed to everything he was trying to do.

In the Spring of 1984 the Session decided to have a mission which would be held in November. The speaker was to be the Rev Jackson Buick. This did not interest me very much.

And so the time came for the mission to commence in November. It was a Friday night which was also our pre-communion service with communion on the following Sunday. As usual I went along to all of these services.

As my wife was the organist, she suggested that I should go along to the service on the Monday night and support the meeting. To keep the peace I went along. During the service that Monday evening I felt as if the speaker and I were the only two people in the church. I was listening. I went back on the Tuesday evening, also on the Wednesday, Thursday and Friday evenings. Each night I felt I wanted to speak to the Rev Buick at the door but did not have the courage. What would my friends in the bowling club think? Has this man Cochrane gone off his head? So, each night I went on home.

On the closing night the Rev Buick described different types of people within the church. He identified three types - (1) those who love the Lord, (2) those who come to church every Sunday faithfully helping out where they can, and (3) those who only use the church when it suits. He explained that the faithful helpers got a mark of forty-five, and those who used the church when it suited them a mark of five. Then after a long pause he said, 'Both have failed!'

When I went home that night all I had in my mind was a voice saying, 'You have failed. You have failed.' Later that night I cried out to the Lord that I was a sinner asking if He would save me. I felt a peace inside me. In the morning I told my wife. She was so pleased for me and said I must let my minister know. This I did. And remember this was the minister that I had opposed at every turn.

My whole life changed. I have never looked back. Because of my change I lost some friends but gained many new friends in Christ Jesus. If you are reading this and feel that because of what your friends might think you cannot come to Jesus, I can assure you that God is good and what He has done for me He can do for you. Life does not automatically become easier once you have trusted Jesus as your Saviour, but He is always there for you in the good times and the more difficult times. He has promised never to leave us nor forsake us.

Yes, we as a family have had our ups and downs but thanks to our Heavenly Father, He has seen us safely through. So I thank God for Jackson Buick and Graham Connor and many, many more who are faithful friends. Life has taken on a new meaning for me as I go about my daily work. I see people around me as important. Yes, His grace is sufficient. What a Saviour!

Charles and Joan Dundee
Recounted by Myself

I came to know Charles and Joan Dundee after I came to the

Craigy Hill congregation at the end of 1970. But in fact I heard about Joan before I arrived; she was, I was told, a great Captain of the 153rd NI Company of the Girls' Brigade. As I have indicated earlier, I was deeply involved with the Girls' Brigade at Northern Ireland Board level, which meant I was a frequent visitor to the Headquarters. In congratulating me upon my call to Craigy Hill the staff there added their commendation of Joan Dundee. I was soon to discover that these words of praise were in no way misplaced.

But the circumstance that set the Dundees - and Joan in particular - in a special category of uniqueness happened after I had left for the prison chaplaincy. One evening in June 1986 after Daisy and I returned to the port of Larne by boat, I called at the Dundee home to collect my car which I had left there while we were visiting our son and daughter-in-law in Birmingham. In the week between our departure and return Joan had heard that there was the possibility of her having cancer. Despite the threat, and in the end the actuality, of cancer - and then its recurrence - with all the treatment and operations involved, Joan lived a full and active life until the end. Sadly, on 10th July 1999 she died at the relatively young age of sixty-one.

Shortly after my installation in Craigy Hill Presbyterian Church I remember calling in the Dundee home on GB business. Though I had gone to see Joan, it was Charlie (as most people called him) who had me pondering. There he was with sleeves rolled up, his substantial frame filling the chair in which he sat. It was our first meeting. In physique and personality he seemed the opposite of what I was. As I left the house I recollect wondering what this man thought of me and what our relationship would be in the days ahead.

At that time the Dundee household consisted of man and wife, and one child - a daughter called Kathryn. Soon a second child - John - was born. He was among the first children that I baptized in Craigy Hill. Both children were brought up to attend Sunday school, Bible class and church and take their part in the church organisations. Indeed as I write John is in charge of the Boys' Brigade Company there.

By profession Joan was a teacher. She held a senior post in Larne High School being responsible for Physical Education and having oversight of other curricular and pastoral assignments. With commitments in church, school and of course home Joan had a very busy schedule, yet in no way could she be accused of neglect. Quite the opposite!

I got to know Joan particularly well - and to appreciate her worth - in her capacity as GB Captain. In Craigy Hill the custom was that the assistant minister accompanied the Boys' Brigade on their annual camp. So each year I went with the Girls Brigade performing the dual role of quartermaster and chaplain. Usually the girls occupied the church halls. I took up residence in the minister's room which became bedroom, study and operations room for the week.

Joan planned camp with the meticulousness of a chess grandmaster. Nothing was left to chance. Every contingency was considered, every eventuality evaluated. Joan aimed to make the holiday as enjoyable as possible. In her view this was best done within a disciplined framework. I admit that I sometimes thought she was almost too strict about certain things but looking back I see that I was wrong and she was right. During the years of my ministry Joan must have arranged camps and expeditions (including those associated with the Duke of Edinburgh awards) for hundreds of girls and I cannot recall one serious mishap.

Throughout camp there was a spiritual undergirding of activities. Joan's personal faith was more evident from her integrity of character, way of life and general demeanour than from a superfluity of theological jargon. Devotions and prayers had their rightful place. Sunday was kept special with the Church Parade taking precedence. There was a refreshing wholesomeness about Joan Dundee's camps. In short they were models of what camps ought to be.

Time also brought me closer to Charlie. He had been on the church committee for several years when in 1977, accompanied by the Clerk of Session, I had to visit the Dundee home. The purpose of our call was to tell Charlie that the votes of the congregation made him, along with others, a nomination for the eldership. We talked over what this meant, but in a week or so there had to be a response.

Our visit was almost over. But in his quiet way Charlie said, 'I do not think I am fit to be an elder.'

'If you are not fit, it's time you were,' I retorted. 'Get down on your knees and trust the Lord.'

We prayed together and turned towards the door. Our short visit was over.

As soon as we left Charlie made his way to the home of another elder, Stewart Hall, with whom he was friendly. The two talked together, Charlie speaking of his reservations about his lack of fitness. Stewart Hall's response was similar to my own with this added comment: 'Whatever is keeping you from being an elder should also keep you from the Lord's Table.'

No doubt Charlie pondered these things in his heart. In any case a work of grace - perhaps as a still small voice - had its effect on Charlie's heart. A few weeks later this strong, burly man took the vows of eldership along with five others. From then on Charlie was a stalwart of the church in both the practical and spiritual spheres.

A few years after I left Larne, as I have already mentioned, cancer entered this home, like it has so many others. Throughout her illness Joan remained outwardly unperturbed, even serene. Eventually she had to give up her work as a teacher but, until a short time before her death, she was active with the Girls' Brigade and attended church twice every Sunday. Instead of being bowed down by her affliction she set about raising money for cancer research. Until her retirement she headed Larne High School's effort in such a way that the school won several awards for its collections. She was also able to empathize with, and give support to, other cancer sufferers.

Joan's last few days were spent in Antrim Area Hospital. Until the end her spirit remained buoyant, her faith secure. She had planned her own funeral service with her minister, the Rev James Johnstone. In a packed church it was a moving yet triumphant service in which I was privileged to share. Among those present to pay their respects were representatives from the Girls' Brigade, including a guard of honour from the Craigy Hill Company. Her son, John, read the Scripture lessons and her son-in-law, Colin Davis (a curate in the Church of England), led in prayers. Sheila Sutter, now a deaconess in First Antrim, read the poem *Death is nothing.*

The first verse of the closing hymn does not quite say it all - nothing could - but it expresses something of how Joan faced suffering.

Father, I place into Your hands
the things I cannot do.
Father, I place into Your hands
the times that I've been through.
Father, I place into your hands
the way that I should go,
for I know I always can trust you.

DAISY BUICK
RECOUNTED BY HERSELF

Unlike my husband, Jackson, I was born into a large family. There were twelve of us, divided nice and evenly: six boys and six girls. Included in this grand total was a set of twin boys who, along with two other boys, died in infancy. I still remember the little white coffins being carried out of our home after a short funeral service. This meant I grew up in a family of five sisters and two brothers.

My father was George Clarke McDowell. My mother's maiden name was Catherine Hewitt. She came from County Cavan.

My father owned a small farm which produced much needed food for the family. To supplement his income he also operated as a carting contractor. With his horse and cart he provided a service for the County Council and for others who required it. Life was far from easy. As children we had to help on the farm after coming home from school. This helped to bind us together as a family, and Dad's diligence, integrity and honesty influenced us for good and for God.

To say that my mother was kept busy is a gross understatement. With a family of our size she had no idle moments. By upbringing and background she was Church of Ireland and, as it happened, Muckamore Parish Church was only a ten minute walk from our home. From time to time mother took us there. She also took us to the Oldstone Sunday School which was connected with First Antrim Presbyterian Church of which we were in fact members. As I look back on my mother's loving care and sacrificial life I am humbled. But it was her love for Christ and His church that made the deepest and most long-lasting impression.

When we were old enough to own bicycles we got more involved in First Antrim. Along with two of my sisters I joined the choir, Girls Auxiliary, Young Peoples' Guild and Christian Endeavour.

I just loved sewing. This led me to becoming an apprentice dressmaker in Bradley's - outfitters who specialized in ladies' fashions. For the first year I left home at 7.30 am and returned at 7.00 pm. My wages were six shillings per week, all of which it took to pay for my weekly bus ticket. You might say I was working for nothing! But I - and others like me - survived and with the passage of time things improved.

As with Jackson, Beth Porter played a part in my spiritual pilgrimage. She invited me to a meeting for young people in the YMCA hall where Lindsay Glegg was the speaker. Before the meeting we shared a meal during which Beth spoke to me about her Christian commitment and personal relationship with her Saviour.

Just now I said I loved sewing. There was something else I loved. I loved dancing. Oh how I loved dancing! Now back in the 1930's and 1940's I think it would be correct to say that there was an innuendo - and sometimes an outright assertion - that Christianity and dancing were incompatible. And here was I, out dancing at least once a week.

To Beth Porter I said, 'I just cannot give up dancing. I think I couldn't give up dancing.'

To profess to be a Christian and continue to live the life I was living would be hypocritical. At that time I fear that dancing had become an idol.

Beth gave me some advice. 'Entrust your life to Christ and He will deal with the dancing if it is a problem.' She had not made giving up dancing a precondition.

Shortly after this my cousin, who belonged to a Brethren Assembly, took me to one their meetings which they called a 'Bible Reading.' It was Easter Monday 1938. I remember very little of what the preacher said, but that very same Monday night I had an extraordinary dream. I dreamed that I was in a hospital bed ...... dying. Although all my friends were round about me, not one of them could do anything for me. Then I saw a figure with outstretched arms. To me this was none other than Jesus Christ. 'Trust me,' He said, 'and you have nothing to fear.'

Then in my dream I trusted Jesus. Suddenly, as is usually the case, I awoke, but the message of the dream lingered on.

Following this dream I attended a CE rally addressed by the Irish CE president, the Rev A E S Strong. Using the chain of office, which he was wearing, he likened the church to the chain and members to the links. The challenge with which we were presented was to decide whether we were weak or strong links or indeed a link at all. This made me think.

I surveyed my past. Traumatic as it had been, the Easter Monday dream had not met my need. It had awakened me to the fact that although I was living a moral life, something - or more accurately someone - was missing. More and more I was realizing the urgency of committing my life to Christ.

By now it was January 1939. The churches in Antrim

had united for a week of prayer. The speaker was my own minister, the Rev M Majury. He spoke on one of the best-known texts in the Bible, '*Marvel not that I say unto thee, Ye must be born again*' (John 3:7). There was neither appeal nor counselling. But that night I trusted Christ as best as I knew how. I then confessed with my lips that I had become a Christian.

Returning to work, I knew myself to be a different person. Change manifested itself in many different - often small - ways. And what about the dancing? The dancing that had become a passion? Beth Porter's words came true. Dancing was no longer a problem in my life. So it has been in the sixty years since; God's grace has been sufficient to help me deal with the problems of life - most of them worse than dancing.

FRANK AND ANN MCKIBBEN
RECOUNTED BY MYSELF

In early September 1963 Daisy and I moved into the Second Newtownards manse in Mark Street just behind the church.

Our first Sunday there turned out to be a beautiful Autumn day. After dinner Daisy, Raymond and I went for a walk along the Crawfordsburn Road. Soon we came upon Frank and Ann McKibben and their son, Gary. There they were sitting on a low wall. They lived in 45 Mark Street on the opposite side from us. We exchanged a few words with them for this was another Newtownards family that we were getting to know.

Four and a half years later I was getting into my car to keep an appointment when who should appear from nowhere but Ann McKibben. Greeting me she said, 'I would like to talk to you.' 'Fine,' I said 'but what would you like to talk about?' Looking me straight in the eye she replied, 'I want to be saved.'

I explained that just then I had an appointment which I had to fulfill. 'But,' I added, I'll call around at Number 45 as soon as I possibly can.'

This I did, sharing with her the Good News of God's way of salvation. I also invited her to join our current communicants' class. Here is the gist of Ann's own explanation for her action.

'One morning,' she said, 'I was doing my household chores with my baby, Janette, crawling around the floor. A thought struck me. If something happened to that child, I reasoned, and she died, she would go to heaven. But if I die, heaven would not be my eternal abode.'

The incident seems banal, even trite. Maybe so, but through it, God spurred Ann into an interest in salvation. Like many young people of her generation, Ann was brought up in a good home, went to Sunday School and church, joined the CE in Greenwell Street and even, at eight years of age, made a profession of faith in Christ. However, as a young married mother, she considered herself a stranger to God's way of salvation.

Now, having had her conscience awakened, she joined

the communicants' class, professed her faith (this time, I think, genuinely) and became more active in the work of the church. A few points from her and her husband's life are relevant here.

After leaving school Ann worked as a waitress in a small café and later in a stitching factory. It was as a waitress that she met her future husband. In March 1959 she and Frank were married in Greenwell Street Presbyterian Church. Their firstborn, Gary, still lives with them; their other children, Janette and Mark, live close by.

Frank remembers how on the first Sunday morning after their marriage his father arrived in 45, Mark Street around 11.00 am. 'Right Frank,' he said, 'it's time we were on our way to the service in Second Newtownards.' Father was trying to make sure that a pattern of church attendance was not broken.

Frank did continue to attend church, indeed was willing to volunteer to join a work party for jobs that needed doing. Of a reserved, quiet disposition, he always found something to do. I cannot imagine him ever being bored. When he was not providing his own amusement he attended football matches or dances, or went out with the lads to have a beer. But for the most part he was fulfilled in his work and family life.

In the 1980s long after I had left the congregation, Second Newtownards introduced Home Bible Study groups. The McKibben homes hosted one of these. Although Frank made no profession of faith, he was not embarrassed to join with Ann in welcoming George Ferguson, the group leader, and others to their home.

In 1987 when the church was preparing for a two-week mission to be conducted by Michael Perrott, Frank was not particularly enthusiastic. 'If these folks expect me to be at a mission every night for two whole weeks,' he ruminated, ''they have another thing coming to them. It's not on.'

Nevertheless on the second Sunday in November - the morning the mission started - Frank was in his pew as usual. Michael Perrott concluded his address by telling of an incident when a lady dropped dead at the end of a service. The story gripped Frank. He was drawn back to the mission that evening, then on the Monday, Tuesday and on each night until the end of the fortnight. Like his wife many years before, Frank was having an encounter with the Living Christ. It ended with him entrusting his life to that Christ. He further followed his wife's footsteps by identifying himself with the Lord's people by coming forward to Communion.

As time passed both Frank and Ann became regulars at the prayer and Bible study meetings. Ann's other interests were with the Girls' Brigade, creche and the Presbyterian Women's Association (PWA). Frank frequented the Men's Fellowship and was on the Church and Missionary committee. Eventually he was ordained to the eldership.

Their home became a sanctuary 'where prayer was wont to be made' and where from Monday to Saturday as well as Sunday they sought the guidance of the Lord for everything in their lives.

Both highlight the principle of Biblical tithing which they practise. As they lay aside one tenth of their finances, they have found the Lord taking over their entire bank account. Even when they have had extra spending and expected their statement to show a debit, they have been surprised - and relieved - to find a credit balance

Through these years Frank and Ann have discovered that in the humdrum, as well as the more obviously spiritual dimension of life, God's grace is not only abundant but abounding.

GEORGE FERGUSON
RECOUNTED BY HIMSELF

As we reflect over the days, months and years of our lives we will, I'm sure, think of many people who have been special to us or who have helped us in some specific way. One person who made a big and important impact in my life was Rev Jackson Buick.

When he arrived in my home congregation of Second Newtownards Presbyterian Church in June 1963 the gospel had never before made any impression on my life although I had been to Sunday School and Church. But very quickly under his ministry the Spirit of God began to convict me and on 16th September, 1963 Mr Buick led me to Christ. From that moment God took control of my life and began to equip me for a life of service for Him.

This began in a small way, firstly by regular attendance at Sunday worship and teaching young children in a Sunday School class which by now was a joy and at which I grew and matured in my faith. The mid-week meetings for prayer and Bible study were a real inspiration to me particularly when I became confident enough to take part in prayer.

In the background Janie, who was a Christian when I met her, kept encouraging me as well. We were privileged to have Rev Buick conduct our marriage and later baptise our three sons. Soon I was elected on to the Church Committee and then served as Treasurer for some fifteen years. Janie was invited to start a Christian Endeavour and was leader for thirty years working with the Juniors during which time I became involved with the Young Peoples' CE.

Six months before Rev Buick left Second Newtownards I was ordained to the eldership. That was in June 1970 and marked a further development of my service for God as I felt God was charging me together with the other believing elders and members of the congregation to see that the work done by God through Rev Buick was continued.

And it was, under the ministry of Rev W J McIlfatrick. God continued to shape me for further service to Him, firstly in leading a Young Peoples' Bible Class which soon developed into an Adult Bible Class. In 1984 I was appointed Clerk of Session shortly before Rev McIlfatrick took ill, an illness which sadly forced him to take early retirement in February 1987. This period was also one in which God continued to prepare me for service for Him as Rev McIlfatrick encouraged me to spend some time at the Belfast Bible College.

During the vacancy in Second Newtownards a planned mission was allowed to continue and under God's guidance I was able to help Mr Perrott in the organisation leading up to it as well as during it. A number of people came to faith in Christ at that Mission and it was a joy to see and experience God at work

The installation of Rev G F McKeown soon followed and this gave me the opportunity to experience the Courts of the Church at work. God was continuing this shaping of my life. The ministry of Rev McKeown was and has continued to be a most effective one. He is an outstanding preacher whom God has used in the salvation of many souls and what a joy it was and is just to be a small part of that. It was in the early days of Rev McKeown's ministry that God gave me a real desire to see souls saved and to confirm to me that He had a job for me to do. In September 1992 I was installed as President of the Irish Christian Endeavour Union and what an honour that was, but I still felt God wanted more from me.

Soon God confirmed to me what it was, what He had been preparing me for. On 2nd June 1993 at a Service of Commissioning in my home Church I was set aside for the task of being Executive Secretary of the Belfast City Mission. The Mission has been at the forefront of evangelism in the City since 1827 and it seeks to reach the poor, the careless and the churchless with the Gospel. With the help of an excellent staff and Mission Board, God has enabled me to lead the Mission through a period of change as it refocuses its vision for reaching out on an ever increasing Godless and secular society. Under God's guidance the Mission has been able to build new halls, refurbish old ones and commence new initiatives for outreach, but above all to keep to its main task of reaching souls for Christ.

It took years for God to prepare me for the task He has now given me. From those early days under the guidance of Rev Buick right up to this very day I can truthfully say that I am where He wants me to be. I thank God for the day He brought me to Himself and began a work in me which has stood the test of time. I would not want to change anything in my life and would encourage you who may be reading this book to surrender your life to Christ and let God do a work in you. '*Wait on the Lord; be strong, and let thine heart take courage; yea, wait thou on the Lord*' (Psalm 27:14).

Chapter 20

Finally and in Conclusion

As in Alice in Wonderland, a preacher sometimes uses a word just to mean whatever he wants it to mean. In sermons, for instance, the word 'lastly' may mean something totally different. The doubly emphatic 'finally and in conclusion' is hardly less ambiguous. However - dare I say it? - I have definitely come to the last, final, concluding chapter.

That I am now reaching the end of the book is a miracle. I have surprised myself. In the very first chapter I wondered if the book would ever get completed. But if it did, I hoped it would 'bring glory to the One who saved me and loosed me from my sins.'

It is not the life stories of either Jackson Buick or the others whose names appear that are important but the grace of the Sovereign Lord in those lives.

As I look back over what I have written and indeed over my eighty years I remember so many others who, because of their faith, made an indelible impression and to whom I am eternally grateful. My indebtedness to the university of experience is immeasurable.

From that 'university' one group, which I have not yet mentioned much, is the **63 Club**. Ten of my contemporaries constituted what might be called a faculty or seminar where we shared and learned from each other. The challenges of preaching and the problems of pastoral ministry were discussed in an atmosphere of comradeship. We were able to rejoice with those that rejoiced and weep with those that wept.

The name **63 Club** was adopted because all the members had taken up their first charge in 1963. Ten times each year, we went around the various manses, wives coming along, too. Nine of us still meet about five times each year; the tenth, the Rev Tom Cuming, joined that Greater Fellowship in Heaven in February 1985 where one day we shall rejoin him.

The **63 Club** was both a place of exposure to necessary criticism by friends and of composure when disappointments and buffetings comes. The political and religious questions of the day were discussed in a good-humoured spirit. In a spirit of humility and trust in God we tried to do the work of the Kingdom in a God glorifying way. If we were in danger of complacency, a member - one in particular - would often keep our feet on the ground by saying (often) 'I object.'

Throughout my life I have enjoyed an excellent bill of health. For this I am thankful to Almighty God. Apart from four days in hospital for a minor complaint as a 9-year-old boy and a sickness certificate for two weeks as an adult I have had no real ailments. A small container would hold my lifetime's medicines. Even at eighty years of age God has granted me the energy and vitality to lead a full and fulfilling life.

By working on this book for the last nine months I have been reminded of how confused many people are about what it means to believe in Jesus. I, too, was once confused. Back in November 1938 my prayer had been, 'I don't know what it is to believe but I believe.' I suppose it was like the prayer of Thomas, *'Lord I believe. Help my unbelief.'*

Though I did not at that time fully understand, my private, personal prayer was a sincere cry from my heart for salvation. Those words of Jesus in John 6:47, *'He that believeth on Me hath everlasting life'* became a reality for me. Throughout the years His grace has kept and sustained me.

Another concern has haunted me through my reflections. It is the matter of assurance which so many people's lack. Often of a humble, gentle disposition they hesitate to acknowledge that they are saved. To profess their Christian faith would, they think, be impertinent, even, as it were, dishonouring to God (for they dwell on their own weaknesses). Such thoughts are contrary to Christ's own words, *'I give unto my sheep eternal life and they shall never perish, neither shall any man pluck them out of my hand.'* (John 10:28). Only by grounding my faith in God's Word have I been able to have assurance in my 63 years as a Christian.

I have often said that I have had a satisfying and purposeful life. If it were possible for me to relive my life, I would not desire its pattern to be much changed. The one persistent temptation has been to be busy in the Master's work yet neglect that personal quiet time with the Master Himself. It is easy to be like Martha - cumbered about much serving - and forget the good part of Mary - to sit at Jesus' feet and hear His word. Yet, to seek the daily advancement of the Kingdom without first - each morning - spending time with the King, is surely a big mistake.

So I conclude with two verses of William Dunn

Longstaff's hymn:

Take time to be holy, speak oft with thy Lord;
Abide in Him always, and feed on His Word;
Make friends of God's children, help those who are weak;
Forgetting in nothing His blessing to seek.

Take time to be holy, let Him be thy Guide;
And run not before Him, whatever betide;
In joy or in sorrow still follow thy Lord,
And , looking to Jesus, still trust in His Word.